Lead Like a Rock Star:
Leadership, Listening, and the Music That Remains

Also, by Dr. Ian D. Russell

Apples for Sale
The Engineer
Five Fish
Transportation Moves You
The Adventures of John James Putter
The International School's Safeguarding Field Guide: Designing Protection That Works in Complex Environments

Lead Like a Rock Star:

Leadership, Listening, and the Music That Remains

Dr. Ian D. Russell

LEAD LIKE A ROCK STAR:
LEADERSHIP, LISTENING, AND THE MUSIC THAT REMAINS

This book is a work of nonfiction based on the author's professional experiences. Certain names and identifying details may have been changed to protect individuals' privacy.

The views expressed in this book are those of the author and do not necessarily reflect the views of any current or former employer or organization with which the author has been affiliated.

Published in the United States of America.

First Edition

ISBN: 978-0-9897805-5-1 (Paperback)
ISBN: 978-0-9897805-4-4 (Hardback)

Cover design by Ian Russell (DallE-30)
Interior design by Ian Russell.

Library of Congress Cataloging-in-Publication Data has been applied for.

DEDICATION

This book is dedicated to Jennifer, Meilan, and Xiana, who have quietly made countless sacrifices along the way to support my life, my music, and my work.

Without a strong supporting band, there is no rock star.

And to the eager young leaders finding their way, take your time. Laugh often. Learn constantly. Retune when needed. Then step back onto the stage and "lead like a rock star."

> "I'm learning all the time. I'm evolving all the time as a human being. I'm getting better, I hope, in all of the important ways."
>
> Neil Peart

CONTENTS

PART III: Harmony and Working with Others

Teams, trust, conflict, culture

PART IV: PERFORMANCE AND VISIBILITY

Courage, front-facing leadership, presence

PART V: LEGACY, MENTORSHIP, AND VOICE

Visibility, Courage, and Consequence

PART VI: REFLECTION, RENEWAL, AND FUTURE LEADERSHIP

Planning, Ethics, AI, and What Remains

ACKNOWLEDGMENTS

I began drafting this book in 2022, and the journey to this final version has taken many unexpected turns. This book was shaped by many people who joined me along my long and unpredictable "world tour," influencing the music of my leadership in ways both subtle and profound.

To the students, colleagues, and leaders I have had the privilege to work for and alongside, thank you. Some of you offered encouragement when I needed confidence. Others offered critique when I needed clarity. Both were gifts. Leadership, like music, improves when someone is willing to listen closely and say, "Play that again… but better."

If it were not for Brenna Creamer, who thought my sketches were awesome and "that I needed to do more with them," both my sketches and this body of work would not have lifted off the ground.

Several leaders helped tune my ear and steady my rhythm: Brent Mutsch, Tim Hansen, Andy Page-Smith, and John Carey. Each had the courage to evaluate my work honestly and hold me accountable to the standards that matter. They did not simply let me play; they helped me learn how to play well.

My father once shared a piece of wisdom that has followed me across every stage of life: "There are no bad experiences, only learning experiences."

Some of those lessons were loud, uncomfortable, even discordant. Yet they became the notes that shaped the melody of who I am becoming.

Music has always been my refuge. The guitar has stayed with me through both harmony and noise. John Kornberg helped me understand that playing in a band is more than sound. It is listening, trust, and shared rhythm, an experience that can lift people in ways few other things can.

Since forming Black Flame in eighth grade, I have seen the parallels between band life and leadership with increasing clarity. Paul, Darby, Jeremy, and Bryan pushed my creativity across Lunchbox, Allen

Wrench and the Broken Strings, and the Leisure Suit Lads, where we collectively wrote more than thirty "hits," at least in our own minds. Both demand listening. Both depend on others. And neither tolerates the illusion that you can lead alone.

And what would any band be without its most loyal fans?

To my wife of more than thirty years, thank you for enduring my antics, my rock star dreams, and my serious side with patience and grace.

To my children: thank you for always making room in the house for just one more guitar. And to my daughter, who once believed that I wrote: "Breakfast at Tiffany's." For one shining moment, I was a legend.

My sister has always supported the work I do. I am grateful for her voice, even if I have not recognized it as often as I should.

Looking back, the truth is simple: every good song is written with others, every band needs people who listen closely, and every leader is shaped by the voices around them. These pages carry many of those voices, and the music they helped create is the leadership I am still learning to play.

A quick note about the illustrations: I created 52 cartoons that inspired the book. I used DALL-E-3 (via Bing/ChatGPT) to give the cartoons a more professional look. Obviously, they did not all make the cut, which was heartbreaking, but a fact of life.

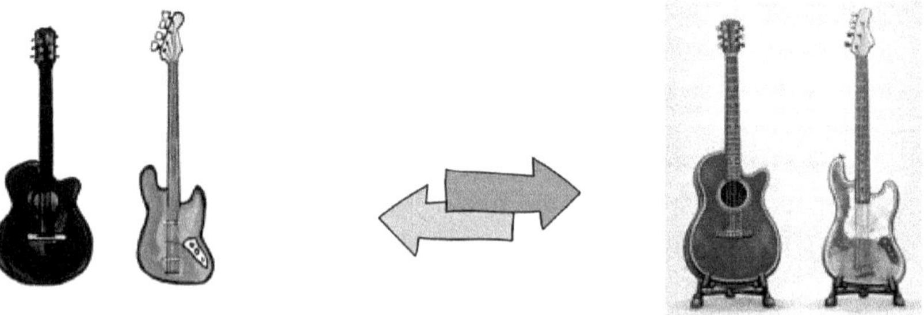

I want to acknowledge the work of Bryn Cavin in helping to edit and shape some of my thinking about the examples I chose to share in the book.

PREFACE:

EVERY SONG BEGINS WITH A NOTE

Every musician recalls the nerves of first picking up an instrument, the buzz of strings, aching fingers, and unsteady timing. Nothing promises future skill. Yet in that uncertain start, one message emerges: Persist. Every struggle is the beginning of a song.

Leadership, like music, begins with an awkward first note, uncertain, unpolished, filled with possibility.

So, when you step into a classroom, meeting, or office, you carry that same mix of composure and nervous energy. The uncertainty lingers just beneath the surface, echoing those tentative first musical notes, as you hope to find a sure footing before you're called to lead on your own.

This book developed as I learned to lead the same way I learned to play music: trying, failing, adjusting, and persevering. Some efforts were harmonious, others not, but both kinds fueled growth. It is a book for those who lead with courage and doubt, who persist when their internal strings are worn and refuse to stop showing up.

Music taught me more about leadership than formal instruction ever could. Persistence outweighs talent, timing is crucial, kindness is transformative, and the truest leaders, like the finest musicians, don't need to be the loudest in the room.

Certain metaphors stayed with me over time. They followed me from role to role and place to place. They surfaced during difficult seasons and clarified moments that felt unmanageable. Eventually, I realized they were not just metaphors. They were the architecture of my leadership.

This book is not a manual. It is not a sermon. It is closer to two people sitting with guitars, tuning slowly, laughing at wrong chord shapes. If something here helps you, take it. If something makes you pause and think, *yes, that's exactly how it feels*, then the book is doing its work.

Before the first chapter begins, take a breath. Tune your instrument. Nothing here requires perfection. Only willingness. Leadership, like music, begins with a single note. This first one is yours.

AUTHOR'S DISCLAIMER:

THE OLDER I GET, THE BETTER I WAS

Nostalgia edits generously, polishing stories, softening edges, and occasionally reshaping memory. For honesty and your psychological comfort, a few clarifications are necessary:

1. **Yes, I may have been less brilliant than I currently recall.** Any early-career performance described here may be more accurately called motivational fiction.
2. **I have made mistakes. Some impressive ones.** If we have worked together previously, thank you for your patience as I tuned my leadership in real time.
3. **If I supported your growth, I'm grateful.** Those moments shaped me as much as they shaped you.
4. **If I missed the mark, I'm sorry.** Not every note landed perfectly. I always intended to get it right, but I know I've missed key changes
5. **I'm still changing my strings.** Daily. Enthusiastically or reluctantly, depending on the week.
6. **Memory may enhance certain stories for dramatic effect.** Names, dates, and hairstyles remain accurate. Emotional tone may shift for narrative coherence.
7. **By reading this book, you agree not to fact-check me with surviving witnesses.** They will not remember it the same way anyway.

Leadership shaped me the long way, the human way, the imperfect way. That is the story I offer here.

THE POWER CHORDS LEADERSHIP MODEL

Every musician learns that simple, powerful elements can create a vast range of sound. In rock music, those elements are power chords, stripped-down, resonant shapes that carry entire songs.

Leadership has its own version of power chords: fundamental disciplines that, like their musical counterparts, shape everything that follows.

Over time, six metaphors surfaced again and again in my work. They appeared in moments of decision, conflict, growth, repair, and consequence. They were not techniques. They were patterns. Together, they form the leadership model that guides this book.

1. **High Notes and Low Notes**: Emotional range. Leadership requires the capacity to move across registers. Authenticity emerges when leaders stop pretending to live in only one tone.
2. **Harmony:** Aligned difference. Strong cultures are not uniform; they are tuned. A band's sound depends on how well its parts listen and adjust to one another.
3. **Know Your Audience**: Situational empathy. The best leaders read the room before they speak to it. Influence begins with awareness.
4. **Set Up Your Own Gear**: Readiness before action. Leaders cannot delegate the internal and practical discipline required to show up grounded, clear, and prepared.
5. **Put Down Your Instruments and Plan**: Reflection during complexity. Leaders must interrupt momentum long enough to restore coherence, realign priorities, and hear the direction beneath the noise.
6. **Face the Music**: Leadership under visibility and consequence. When tension rises or impact becomes public, leaders stand in the moment, absorb scrutiny, own their decisions, and respond with integrity.

These six strings move deliberately: from inner tone to relational alignment, to disciplined preparation, to public courage. They unfold progressively throughout this book, forming a leadership arc that culminates in visibility and consequence.

Each string carries tension. Leadership requires learning how to tune and play all six.

Before any leader plays a first real chord, they must pick up the instrument, awkwardly, bravely, imperfectly. Part I begins with identity, wiring, and the early notes that shape every leader's sound. Turn the page. It is time to begin tuning.

PART I: PICKING UP THE INSTRUMENT

Finding Your Sound: Identity, Beginnings, Foundations

“Leadership is not about resolving tension between who you are. It is about learning how to play both notes without losing the song.”

Ian D. Russell

CHAPTER 1:
Every Song Begins with a Note!

Every leadership story begins long before a title or a job description. It starts in quiet, uncertain moments, when you first step forward and hope no one can hear how nervous you are. It is not so different from the moment a young musician picks up a guitar for the first time. Fingers ache. The sound is more ambition than artistry. Still, something stirs, a small whisper of possibility: *Keep going. There's something here worth pursuing.*

Looking back at my early leadership, I don't remember confidence or clarity. I remember that old guitar, heavy, awkward, but compelling. My first attempts were uneven.

"Smoke on the Water" (Deep Purple, 1975) never sounded so disgraced, full of good intention, more noise than music. But something mattered, even if I didn't understand it: the decision to try. Not to succeed. Not to impress. Simply to begin.

Leadership starts not with brilliance, but with willingness. As you enter your first classroom, staff meeting, or difficult conversation, you carry your history, temperament, hopes, and insecurities. Already, whether you realize it or not, you are shaping a tone. Some begin with bold, confident chords, others with quiet, reflective notes. Most find themselves between the two, adjusting and discovering what feels most authentic.

Beginning before you feel ready is not a flaw; it is a rite of passage. No one steps into leadership fully formed. You discover yourself by doing, by misjudging, saying too much or too little, stepping forward too quickly or hesitating too long, and by learning the difference. Musicians call this *developing an ear*. Leaders learn to develop their voice.

Early struggles are not proof of inadequacy, although they often feel that way. They show that you are stretching into new territory. In those first attempts, you learn how you respond under pressure, how you repair mistakes, how you adapt when plans collapse, and how much you care about those depending on you. These moments shape leadership long before awards or promotions appear.

Leadership identity takes shape when you realize you are choosing rather than just reacting. Like a musician picking a note, you decide how to show up, listen, and set the emotional tone. You ask: What sound do I want to bring into the world? Not what others expect, but what reflects your values, your wiring, and how you believe people should be treated.

I believe leadership is more musical than mechanical. It relies on timing and presence as much as clarity and strategy. Skilled leaders notice subtle shifts in how musicians perceive changes in pitch. They know when to lean in and when to step back.

They understand that tone, pauses, and restraint shape atmosphere as much as words.

Just as musicians change strings, shift keys, and rework melodies, leaders evolve. The note you start with does not limit you. What matters is the note you choose next. The first sound introduces you. The sound you grow into becomes your signature.

This chapter is the first note of the book. Your leadership story has many notes ahead, high and low, practiced and improvised. What matters is the willingness to begin, even if the first sound is imperfect. It always is. The beginning is not meant to impress, but to be honest.

Every song begins with a note.
Every leader begins by deciding to try.
This is where we start

“The challenge is to keep learning.”

Yo-Yo Ma

CHAPTER 2:
Humans Are Jazz, Not Marching Bands

If schools were simple, leadership would be simple. People would move in predictable lines, follow steady rhythms, and respond reliably to direction. It would feel like conducting a marching band, orderly, synchronized, tidy in form and outcome. But anyone who has led a classroom or school team, or lined up children after recess, knows this is not how humans work in their daily lives. They do not march. They improvise. Humans are jazz.

I learned this slowly. Early in my career, like many educators, I expected clear rhythms and steady tempos. I believed that careful planning, strong communication, and good routines would naturally produce compliance. What I encountered instead was something far more complex and far more human. Students arrived each morning moving to different tempos: one energetic, one anxious, one hopeful, one exhausted, one holding something unspoken. Adults brought their own melodies too, shaped by history, fear, strength, and the residue of past workplaces.

A school is a living ensemble of shifting rhythms. No two days sound the same. No two people resonate alike. Leadership in this environment is less about issuing commands and more about listening for cues, about knowing how and when to enter the music.

Jazz musicians understand this instinctively. They know structure matters but feel matters too. Sheet music offers only part of the truth; the rest must be sensed in real time. They anticipate shifts, lean into tension, and trust that dissonance can resolve into something honest. They adapt without losing the coherence of the whole.

This is leadership.

It took me years to see people this way. Early on, I mistook fear for resistance, overwhelm for disengagement, silence for agreement, and confidence for comprehension. Slowly, and sometimes uncomfortably, I learned that people are layered and shaped by contexts I could not see. Their reactions were not always about me, and their behavior rarely told the full story.

Once I accepted this complexity, my leadership softened, not in strength, but in posture. I listened more carefully. I paid attention to energy beneath words, to pauses, to the practiced professionalism of people trying to hold themselves together. I learned that leading people requires musical sensitivity, a willingness to hear the notes within the chords.

When you understand that humans are jazz, you stop expecting perfect synchronization. You stop taking differences personally. You begin to hear how rich a team can sound when people bring their true tone. Structure still matters, perhaps more than ever, but it becomes the frame, not the cage. Boundaries exist not to restrict people, but to create the safety needed for complex, creative work.

I have seen the difference this makes in meetings where frustration was really a plea for help; in coaching conversations where refusal masked embarrassment; in conflicts fueled by ghosts from previous workplaces. When you see people as jazz, you approach them with curiosity rather than certainty. You ask different questions. You enter conversations ready to learn, not to win.

Leadership deepens when you embrace complexity. Chaos is not always dysfunction; sometimes it is people finding their place in the ensemble. Harmony is not the absence of tension; it is the ability to integrate difference into something coherent. Your task is not to enforce a single tempo, but to guide people toward shared purpose while honoring shifting rhythms.

Human beings are improvisational by nature. Leading them requires patience, empathy, and adaptability without self-erasure. It requires stepping into the music and listening beneath the surface, because people "do not march. They improvise. Humans are jazz, a reality consistently misunderstood in systems that privilege uniformity over internal complexity" (Cain, 2012).

We may try to arrange schools like marching bands, but the truth will always be jazz. Once we accept that, leadership becomes more accurate, more generous, and far more human.

“Better sound does not come from playing harder. It comes from knowing when to change the strings.”

Unattributed

CHAPTER 3:
Change Your Strings

There comes a moment in every guitarist's life when the sound no longer rings the way it used to. At first, the change is subtle, a dullness in tone, a faint loss of brightness, a dissatisfaction you cannot quite name. You keep playing, telling yourself it is fine, that you can get through one more rehearsal, one more song. But the instrument knows the truth before you do. The strings have worn thin. It is time to change them.

Leadership reaches this moment too, though it rarely announces itself clearly. Instead, it arrives quietly. You find yourself discouraged by things that once energized you. You snap when you mean to breathe. The pace feels heavier, even though the work has not changed. You are recognizing yourself less and less in the tone you bring to each interaction. Nothing is broken, but something is off.

The first time I felt this as a young administrator, I ignored it. I believed grit meant pushing harder, and resilience meant enduring without complaint. I worked later, planned more, and forced myself to keep strumming tired patterns. The harder I pressed, the duller the sound became. I was no longer the leader I intended to be, and my colleagues felt it before I admitted it.

Changing your strings is the decision to renew before exhaustion becomes identity. Guitarists know that fresh strings do not change the instrument; they restore its voice. Leadership renewal works the same way. It is not reinvention. It is maintenance.

Renewal is difficult because it requires stepping back from the very work that makes you feel indispensable. You cannot retune a string while it is under constant tension. Leaders cannot restore clarity while continually resisting the demands placed upon them. The pressure to remain tight, responsive, and resonant makes pause feel irresponsible, but tone always degrades when maintenance is postponed.

I have known leaders who never took a breath. They carried every crisis, answered every email, absorbed the emotional weight of entire communities. Their dedication was undeniable. So was their exhaustion. Over time, they began responding from a place of depletion rather than clarity. Their leadership remained competent, but the edges frayed. People felt it, even when they could not name it.

Fresh strings change resonance. Fresh clarity changes influence. Renewal can be rest, family, or conversation with someone who helps you see yourself again. It can be therapy. It can be professional, reading, learning, or taking a walk around school to remember what possibility feels like. Sometimes it is as simple as pushing back from the desk and walking among students at recess, letting their joy recalibrate you.

Renewal often arrives quietly. I remember sitting with a teacher who had been carrying a relentlessly challenging class. Strong. Creative. Steady. That day her voice trembled as she said, "I don't know if I can keep doing this." In that moment, she was not a staff member reporting to me. She was a human being worn thin by work she loved.

Instead of offering solutions, I asked, "Tell me, what feels broken right now?"

Everything shifted. She exhaled, and so did I. Her honesty revealed a truth I had been ignoring. I had been leading from urgency rather than compassion. I had forgotten that leadership is not about fixing people, but about staying long enough for them to feel seen.

Changing your strings is not dramatic. It is deliberate. It is a quiet act of stewardship, of your work, your relationships, and your well-being. You do not wait for the string to snap. You change it when the sound begins to fade.

Renewal is not weakness. It is wisdom. Unfortunately, it took me years to hear that. In my defense, I could not yet hear how my own strings sounded.

Fresh strings will not play the music for you, but they will help you find your voice again. And leadership, real leadership, depends on that voice being alive, honest, and fully yours.

"The beautiful thing about learning is nobody can take it away from you."

B.B. King

CHAPTER 4:
Six Strings or Four

One of the most liberating truths in both music and leadership is that not every instrument needs the same number of strings to make something meaningful. A six-string guitar offers range, versatility, and the ability to carry melody and harmony at once. A four-string bass offers depth, grounding, and quiet authority. Neither is superior. They simply contribute differently, and different is essential.

It took me years to accept this lesson in leadership. Early on, I believed great leaders possessed every skill, charisma, confidence, decisiveness, creativity, emotional intelligence, strategic insight, and the ability to read a room instantly. I watched colleagues who seemed naturally gifted in areas where I felt less sure, and I carried the belief that leadership required a suitcase full of talents I wasn't sure I had.

The longer I worked in schools, the clearer it became that excellence in leadership is not about having everything. It is about understanding your instrument, your ways of thinking, your strengths, your temperament, and learning to play it well.

Some leaders naturally carry the six-string range. They fill a room with energy, ideas, and bold direction. Others lead like the bass: steady, calm, grounding, reliable when everything else feels unpredictable. Some step forward with melody; others lay the foundation that lets everyone else shine. Leadership does not come in one shape or tone. The power comes from fit, not from volume or visibility alone (Cain, 2012).

Over time, I realized that comparing myself to other leaders was like a bass player comparing their instrument to a lead guitarist's and wondering why their own sound wasn't brighter. A bass isn't meant to be brighter. It's meant to be deeper. The moment you understand that difference, leadership shifts from self-doubt to clarity.

I have worked with leaders who had a quieter presence but unmistakable impact. Colleagues sought them out during conflict because they listened without judgment. They didn't need to be the loudest voice in the room, but they were often the most trusted. I have also worked with leaders whose energy filled every corner of a building, bringing momentum and possibility wherever they went. Their range created lift. Their presence set direction.

Both types were necessary. Neither needed to copy the other.

A school is an ensemble with many roles: visionaries, stabilizers, collaborators, analysts, encouragers, challengers, and quiet anchors who hold people steady. When leaders try to perform in another musician's signature, the sound becomes strained, sometimes even insincere. When they embrace their natural instrument, their leadership becomes clearer, more authentic, and far more sustainable.

I remember a teacher I once mentored who constantly compared herself to a colleague who was charismatic, theatrical, and wildly popular with students. "I can't do what she does," she told me. "I don't have that spark." But what she did have was equally powerful: she created calm in children who carried anxiety, noticed quiet pain, and made overwhelmed students feel safe. She was a bass player, grounding the room without demanding attention. Her impact ran deep.

When she finally understood that her strength wasn't supposed to look like someone else's, her confidence grew. Her teaching didn't change dramatically, but her identity did. She began to lead from her center instead of chasing someone else's range.

The same shift happens in leadership. When you recognize your unique tone, your "six strings" or your "four", you stop trying to perform and start trying to contribute. You become less interested in covering every role and more interested in playing your role well. You begin to understand that a team doesn't need twelve people with the same strengths. It needs a balanced chord.

A six-string guitar without a bass feels incomplete. A bass without melody lacks dimension. A team where everyone tries to sound like the same kind of leader: bold, loud, extroverted, endlessly energetic, will miss the quieter wisdom that gives depth to the work. A team of only quiet leaders will miss the propulsion needed during big transitions. The ensemble needs every voice.

Your job is not to be everything. Your job is to know your instrument's part and play it with integrity.

The number of strings you bring into a leadership space doesn't determine your value. The sincerity of your sound does. Some leaders build momentum; others build trust. Some create spark; others create steadiness. Every contribution matters when it fits the person offering it. The music works when each person plays the instrument they were meant to play.

"Success is not what you have, but who you are."

Amy Grant

CHAPTER 5:
The Opening Act

It is the moment before the main set, when the stage lights feel too bright, and the room feels too large. You hope the audience is generous. You hope you don't forget the first chord. You hope you sound like someone worth listening to. Mostly, you hope you belong on that stage at all.

The beginning of any leadership journey feels like an opening act, full of anticipation, full of doubt, and full of the quiet hope that the work you are about to do matters to someone other than yourself. Those early moments are often misunderstood. They are not polished displays of expertise. They are raw. They reveal vulnerability long before they reveal capability.

My own opening act began long before I was given a title. It began when I was a young teacher with far more questions than answers. I remember standing in front of my first classroom, trying to look composed while my mind felt like a crowded soundcheck: too many inputs, too much noise, too many knobs I didn't yet know how to turn. I wanted to do well, but I also wanted to hide the fact that I didn't yet know what "doing well" meant.

What I didn't understand then was that those early, awkward moments were shaping me more deeply than the success that came later. The opening act is where you learn who you are when no one is clapping yet. It is where you decide whether you lead from authenticity or performance. It is where you make peace with the truth that leadership implies visibility, whether you sought it or not.

The opening act also tests your relationship with failure, not the dramatic, public kind, but the small failures no one else sees: the lesson that fell apart halfway through, the parent conversation that left you unsettled, the meeting where you spoke too quickly or not quickly enough. These moments don't end your career. They begin shaping it. They teach you what needs adjusting, strengthening, and letting go.

Over time, I learned that the discomfort of the opening act isn't a sign that you shouldn't be on the stage. It's a sign that you're paying attention. Leaders who feel nothing at the beginning often hear nothing later. Nerves, self-doubt, hesitation, these are often signals of care. They keep you humble enough to learn and brave enough to keep stepping forward.

There is also a kind of beauty in the opening act that becomes harder to access later. When you are new, you listen differently. You observe more closely. You feel a sense of responsibility with an electric sincerity. You haven't yet been dulled by routine or hardened by experience. Your leadership tone is still forming, and its early shape, compassion, attentiveness, desire to serve, often becomes the truest part of later practice.

I have heard musicians say the opening act reveals whether a band will last. Not because the performance is perfect, but because it shows whether the musicians are playing out of ego or out of love for the sound they are making together. Leadership shows the same pattern. The leaders who endure are not the ones who begin perfectly. They are the ones who begin honestly, aware of their gaps, committed to growing into responsibility.

What I eventually discovered is that the opening act never fully goes away. Each new role, each new school, each new challenge brings you back under the lights, trying to find your footing. With time, your relationship to that moment changes. You begin to understand the audience isn't waiting to judge you; they are hoping you will find the right chord. Your team, your students, and your colleagues want you to succeed because it helps them succeed too. They are not critics. They are co-creators of the environment you are trying to build.

Leadership becomes more sustainable once you stop trying to survive the opening act and start honoring it. It reminds you of purpose before expectations get heavy. It is the place where sincerity outweighs polish and intention matters more than technique.

When someone new asks, quietly, "Does it always feel this uncertain in the beginning?" you'll be able to smile and say, "Yes, it does. That's how you know you're paying attention."

“Once you get your guitar, you never forget it. It becomes a part of you.”

Willie Nelson

CHAPTER 6:
The First Guitar You Ever Loved

Every guitarist remembers their first instrument. It may not have been beautiful. It may not have been very good. But it was yours. The connection had little to do with craftsmanship, tone, or price. It had everything to do with the moment in your life when it arrived, with who you were becoming, with what you needed, and with how it made you feel.

My first guitar was far from impressive. The neck was slightly warped, the action too high, and the strings felt like thin wires determined to punish every mistake. It fell out of tune halfway through "Stairway to Heaven" (the second song every budding rockstar tries to learn), but none of that mattered. When I held it, I felt a steady pull toward possibility. It invited me into a version of myself I didn't yet know how to inhabit. I didn't have language for that then. I just knew that when I played, no matter how poorly, the world felt slightly larger. In my mind, I was the rockstar still-to-come.

Leadership has its own "first guitar": the moment, role, or person that awakens something in you and leaves a mark you carry for the rest of your career. It's rarely glamorous. It's often small. But it changes the architecture of how you think about people, responsibility, and the sound you want to bring into a community.

For many leaders, that "first guitar" is a mentor who took them seriously before they had earned the right to be taken seriously. For others, it's a classroom, a team, a coaching group, or a job they stumbled into without realizing it would shape their purpose. Sometimes it's a moment that lasts only seconds: a student confiding something heartbreaking, a colleague showing unexpected trust, a parent offering gratitude you didn't feel you deserved. Whatever it is, the experience anchors itself to your identity. It becomes the first resonance of who you might become.

I didn't know it then, but my cheap guitar was teaching me more about leadership than music. It taught me patience with imperfection, mine and the worlds. It taught me how to stay with something long enough to move past frustration into understanding. It taught me that progress isn't visible at first, and that the only way to get better is to keep showing up, even when everything feels out of tune.

Perhaps most importantly, it taught me affection. You don't love your first guitar because of its technical quality. You love it because it met you at a formative time. Leadership is rooted in that same kind of affection: devotion to the people you serve, the community you build with them, and the work that gives your days meaning. The music comes later. Love comes first.

Years after I traded that guitar for better instruments, I still think about the way it shaped my hands and my ear. Every callus and every mistake was part of my education. I learned not just how to play, but how to learn, how to stay in discomfort long enough for something new to emerge. Leadership requires the same tolerance for friction, the same willingness to grow through it rather than around it.

Most leaders can name their "first guitar." It's the memory they return to when the work becomes overwhelming. It's the reminder that leadership didn't begin with competence; it began with curiosity. It began with hope. It began with someone, or some experience, quietly saying, *this might be part of who you are.*

You may outgrow the role, the organization, or the early version of yourself, but you never lose the imprint. You never forget the moment you realized you could bring something meaningful to others, not because you were fully prepared, but because you were willing to begin.

Your first guitar doesn't define you.
It introduces you to yourself.

In the end, leadership grows out of that introduction: the recognition that you have something worth offering, and that the world is full of people who just might need the sound only you can make.

“You don’t need to know all the chords. You just need to know a few good ones.”

Keith Richards

CHAPTER 7:
Learning the F Chord

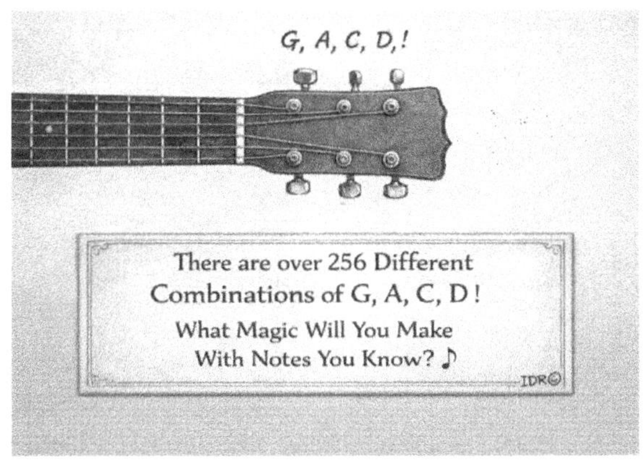

There are certain chords beginning guitarists dread most, and the F chord sits near the top of the list. It demands more strength than you think you have, and more precision than you feel ready for. It requires a full barre across the first fret, which means every finger must press down with commitment, even when your hand feels unprepared for the task. No amount of wishing or shortcutting makes it easier. You work through the discomfort until your muscles catch up to your intention.

The first time I tried to play an F chord, the sound was terrible: muted, buzzy, thin, and wildly inconsistent. My hand cramped. My forearm burned. I wondered how anyone had ever managed to make that shape cleanly. Watching skilled players do it effortlessly felt almost unfair. They made it look natural, even though everything in my body insisted it was anything but.

Over time, I learned a truth that should be obvious but rarely feels that way in the moment: every guitarist has suffered through the F chord at first. No one arrives with strength already built. The ease you see in others is the product of repetition, failure, and thousands of imperfect attempts. When beginners quit early, it is rarely due to lack of talent. It is because they mistake difficulty for impossibility.

This is also the story of adolescence.

Working with young people taught me as much about the F chord as music ever did. Teenagers move through the world with their hands on a fretboard; they are still learning to manage their emotions, social lives, and neurology. Their brains are rewiring at a remarkable pace, pruning old pathways and building new ones that will carry them into adulthood. Emotions run louder. Reactions land sharper. Confidence is more fragile than most of them will admit. Many adolescents live in a constant state of learning the F chord, pushing through experiences that feel too big, too complex, too demanding, or too uncomfortable.

I remember a student who once told me, in a moment of honest frustration, "It feels like everything is too much." And it was. Not because he was weak or unmotivated, but because adolescence asks young people to make sense of the world while still building the internal structures required to carry it. Their version of an F chord might be friendship drama, academic pressure, identity questions, or a family conflict for which they do not yet have language. To adults, these challenges can look small. To teenagers, they are mountain ranges.

As educators and leaders, we sometimes forget how hard the F chord really is once we have learned to play it. We forget the sting of early attempts. We forget how exposed it felt to try to learn something that was supposed to be "basic," yet felt impossible. We forget that what is easy now was once the very thing that made us want to quit.

Leaders face new F chords, too. There are moments in our careers when we are asked to step into roles, we do not yet feel strong enough for, or to make decisions under pressure we do not yet know how to handle. The discomfort is not a sign that you are failing; it is a sign that you are stretching. Adults just disguise their struggle more elegantly than adolescents do. We hide hand cramps behind calm expressions and buzzing strings behind practiced language.

With time, the F chord becomes second nature. The hand that once trembled gains confidence. The sound becomes full and clean. You begin to forget that it ever felt impossible, but that memory matters because it teaches humility. It reminds you to be patient with others and with yourself. It helps you respect the learning curve hidden inside every person's journey, no matter their age or role.

The F chord taught me more about leadership than any promotion ever did. It taught me that difficulty is not a verdict; it is an invitation. It taught me that persistence can outlast talent. It taught me that growth often looks like failure until suddenly it does not. And it taught me that supporting others requires remembering the weight of your own early struggles, not minimizing them once they are behind you.

Most importantly, it taught me to see students and colleagues with more compassion. Everyone is learning some version of the F chord. Everyone is working through something that feels just a little too big for them. Sometimes what people need is not a reminder to be better, but reassurance that the stretch they feel is normal and temporary.

The F chord eventually becomes playable. Beautiful, even. But only because you keep trying long after the moment you want to quit. Leadership, like music, grows from that quiet willingness to press the string again.

INTERLUDE:
My Father's Guitar Case

There was a guitar in our home that my father never played. It moved with us from place to place, tucked into corners, leaning against walls, sometimes half-hidden behind boxes. The latches were scuffed. The edges were worn. It looked like it had a story, but no one ever stopped long enough to tell it. My father was not a musician. He never sat down with the instrument inside, never treated it as anything other than one more object to move when we packed up and started again.

For him, the guitar case was background, part of the scenery of family life, no more important than a piece of furniture. For me, it was something else entirely.

I would look at that case and feel an odd pull toward it, as if it were a door no one had tried in a long time. I imagined what might happen if it were opened, if the guitar inside were tuned, if someone, maybe me, decided to learn how to play. I did not have language for it then, but I sensed the case represented everything that could be if someone was willing to lift the lid and begin.

In that way, the guitar case became a quiet symbol of possibility. It did not match my father's relationship with it. The case did not hold the same meaning for him as it did for me. He would never have seen in it what I saw: an invitation.

Maybe that is part of leadership, recognizing invitations that others walk past. Seeing potential where others see clutter or inconvenience. Feeling drawn to a possibility that has not yet been claimed. The guitar case reminded me, even as a young person, that there are things in our lives that could come alive if we are willing to pick them up. That is what these first chapters have been about: the beginning of a voice before it becomes a role.

I have often thought about that difference between us. My father's influence shaped my understanding of leadership: his steadiness, his humility, his commitment to the people in his care. But the guitar case was mine. It was my way of imagining another kind of voice, another way of showing up in the world.

I learned much later that the case was a memento my father bought in Tijuana, Mexico, the year after he married my mother, a marriage that lasted more than sixty years. The case, quiet and unopened, held a future no one had chosen yet. In time, I opened it and played the nylon-string mariachi guitar until my fingers bled in the summer of '69. I began the slow, imperfect work of learning to play.

In many ways, that was the moment my leadership life began, not when I first stood at a podium or took on a title, but when I decided to open something that had been closed and see what might be possible.

My father's guitar case was never really about my father. It was about the part of me that looked at something unused and heard, very faintly, the sound of what could be.

I still have that guitar. It needs repair and care, and I look forward to tending to it. Some beginnings last a lifetime.

PART II: Growth, Practice, and Resilience

Learning the Craft That Makes Your Sound Reliable: Failure, courage, authenticity, skill-building

"If I don't practice one day, I know it; two days, the critics know it; three days, the public knows it."

Jascha Heifetz

One of the greatest violinists in history.

CHAPTER 8:
Practice and Rehearsal

There is a quiet, humbling truth all successful musicians must eventually accept: most of the work happens when no one is watching. Performances are public, but practice is private. Rehearsal is where real progress occurs, slowly, unevenly, and often without any visible sign that you are improving. It is the daily return to the same chord shape, the same riff, the same transition, until your hands finally understand what your mind has been asking them to do.

Leadership grows in the same private spaces.

Long before your decisions become visible to a team, long before your presence shapes a room, long before you speak words that matter, you rehearse. You rehearse patience, clarity, empathy, restraint, timing, and courage. You practice staying steady when you want to rush and listening when you want to interrupt. You practice standing firm in your values even when doing so creates discomfort. None of this is glamorous. Most of it is invisible. But it becomes the foundation of everything that follows.

I learned this first through music. In my early attempts at guitar, I imagined skill would come from inspiration. I thought I would sit down, feel something, and suddenly the music would flow. But nothing flowed. My hands needed repetition, not passion. The more I practiced, the more honest the sound became. I began to understand that inspiration often arrives while you are working, not before. Rehearsal is the soil from which confidence grows.

The same principle held when I stepped into leadership. I quickly discovered that the moments where I felt most prepared, the difficult conversations, the thoughtful responses, the clear decisions, were almost always the byproducts of small, private practice. I had been rehearsing without realizing it: watching good leaders, absorbing lessons from mistakes, noticing how people responded to tone and timing, learning what calmed a room and what fractured it.

Practice is not only repetition. It is a reflection. It is the drive home when you replay a conversation and realize what you would do differently next time. It is the morning when you set an intention for how you want to show up. It is the acceptance that you are not finished, not perfect, and not supposed to be. You are learning an instrument that demands lifelong rehearsal.

One thing that distinguishes strong leaders from struggling ones is their relationship to practice. Some interpret it as evidence of inadequacy. Others see it as stewardship, an act of care for the people who will someday depend on their clarity. Leadership, as John Maxwell argues, is not built in moments of visibility, but in the accumulation of daily disciplines practiced long before anyone notices the results (Maxwell, 2007). The leaders who endure are rarely the ones with effortless talent. They are the ones who keep returning to the work, even when it feels slow.

Schools, perhaps more than any other environment, require constant rehearsal. Each day brings a new tempo, new dynamics, and new challenges that test your tone. You cannot rely on yesterday's skills to meet today's demands. You adapt, refine, and make small adjustments that no one else notices, but that slowly reshape your leadership into something steadier.

Rehearsal also teaches humility. It strips away the illusion that competence is innate or permanent. It reminds you that even your strengths require tending, and it helps you understand students and colleagues who are also practicing, learning new emotional chords, new social scales, new professional riffs. When you are aware of your own rehearsal, you become gentler with theirs.

What I love most about practice is that it has no applause. It belongs only to you. You become a better leader not because an audience is watching, but because the work matters enough to keep shaping your craft. When the moment comes that someone needs you, when a child breaks down, when a parent is frightened, when a colleague is overwhelmed, when the community looks to you for stability, you will have something steady to offer, not because you were born with it, but because you rehearsed it long before the moment arrived.

Music taught me there is no shortcut to skill. Leadership taught me there is no shortcut to trust. Both grow through the same ritual: showing up, practicing your part, and honoring the quiet hours away from the spotlight.

Practice is not preparation for leadership.
It is leadership. How you rehearse is how you will lead.

"The note I thought was wrong… suddenly I realized it wasn't wrong. It was what I did afterwards that made it right."

Herbie Hancock

CHAPTER 9:
You Never Play Your First Song Perfectly

No one forgets the first time they try to play an actual song on guitar. After days or weeks of practicing chords in isolation, C, G, D, maybe the dreaded F, you finally decide to put them together. The moment feels ceremonial. You sit up straighter. You take a breath. You expect something like music to emerge.

And then it doesn't.

Your fingers hesitate. The chords buzz. The tempo wobbles. The transitions fall apart. Halfway through, you mutter something frustrated under your breath and start again from the beginning. It feels like the song is fighting you, refusing to take shape. You are certain you are doing everything wrong, even though you do not yet know what "right" is supposed to feel like.

Every guitarist has lived this moment. You never play your first song perfectly. You are not supposed to.

It takes time before your hands trust themselves. It takes repetition for your ear to recognize your own voice. It takes humility to listen closely enough to adjust what is not working. The beauty is not in how well you play the song, but in the fact that you try.

Leadership has its own first songs: your first staff meeting, your first difficult parent conversation, your first time guiding a team through tension, your first moment realizing that your words, your tone, your timing, your presence changed the room in ways you did not anticipate. You do not play these moments perfectly. You may say too much or not enough. You may second-guess yourself afterward. You may walk away convinced someone else could have done it better.

Perfection has never been the point. Practice has.

I used to believe mistakes in leadership were evidence that I was not ready. When something went poorly, I took it as proof that someone else should have been in the room instead of me. Over time, I realized that leadership, especially in schools, is more like a long improvisational performance than a rehearsed concerto. You respond in real time to emotion, personality, crisis, and context. There is no perfect script. There is only your capacity to stay present and learn from each imperfect attempt.

What helped me most early on was not confidence. I did not have much of that. It was the recognition that everyone I admired had their own catalogue of imperfect first songs. Mentors had missteps. Skilled leaders had awkward beginnings.

Even the people who seemed effortless had seasons where nothing they tried landed the way they hoped.

They grew because they kept playing.

There is an honesty in imperfection that people trust more than flawless execution. When you try, recover, adjust, and try again, you show your team what resilience looks like. You often, unintentionally, teach students that mistakes are part of the mastery process. You model courage, the kind that does not depend on getting everything right.

The first song may not sound good, but it introduces you to a truth you cannot learn any other way: you survive it. You get another chance. Each time you return, each time you attempt the conversation again or reenter the room, you get slightly better. Your tone softens. Your timing sharpens. Your confidence settles into something less dramatic but more real.

I have never known a leader who played their early songs perfectly, but I have known many who played them with sincerity, attention, and a willingness to grow. That willingness becomes the quiet foundation of everything that follows.

The first song does not have to be perfect.
It only has to be attempted.

Sometimes it really does take five seconds of courage.
Everything after depends on that beginning.

“Honor your mistakes as a hidden intention.”

Brian Eno

Inventor of ambient music.

CHAPTER 10:
Don't Dwell on the Missed Notes

Inevitably, you will eventually miss a note so loudly, so obviously, that it feels like the entire room must have noticed it. You wince. You tense. You wait for the music to fall apart. But often, the people listening do not react. The music continues. The performance goes on. The missed note dissolves into the larger sound.

It took me years to learn what musicians learn early: the note you dwell on lasts longer than the note you miss.

When I first started leading teams, every misstep felt catastrophic. A poorly phrased sentence, an email sent too quickly, a decision that created confusion, a conversation that drifted off course. I replayed each one long after everyone else had moved on. I carried them as proof that I was not ready, not good enough, lacking something essential. I told myself dwelling was responsible, that scrutinizing every error meant I cared.

But caring is different from clinging.

Most people do not remember your mistakes the way you do. They remember your presence. They remember how you made them feel. They remember whether you listened, whether you took responsibility, and whether you returned with more clarity and intention.

Leaders often hold themselves to a level of perfection they would never demand from anyone else. We forgive others easily while holding ourselves hostage to every imperfection. Leadership is rarely undone by one missed note. It falters when leaders become so consumed by errors that they stop playing altogether. They hesitate, retreat, or lead from fear rather than from authenticity.

I saw this clearly the first time I played guitar in front of a small group. About halfway through the song, my fingers landed wrong. The chord clattered out in a way that made a few people glance up. My instinct was to stop, apologize, start over, and erase the moment. But the listeners did not need perfection; they needed continuity. So, I kept playing. The moment passed. The song recovered. Later, someone told me they admired that I didn't freeze. The mistake they barely noticed had been the moment I couldn't forget.

Schools are filled with opportunities to miss notes. A student walks in carrying something heavy that you didn't see. A parent meeting goes sideways. A conversation that should have been gentle comes out too sharply. A decision made in good faith doesn't land the way you hoped. These are human realities of leadership, not its disqualifiers. You cannot lead people well if you expect every note to ring perfectly.

When I look back, the moments that shaped me were rarely the ones where everything went smoothly. There were moments when I missed something, an emotional cue, a detail, a timing shift, and had to recover with grace. There were moments when I learned to acknowledge my mistakes without letting them define me. There were moments when I stopped demanding flawlessness and focused instead on repair.

I still remember a small lesson from my early years in the classroom. I had just finished writing my first report card and made a mistake I still catch myself making: I mixed up "their" and "there." Principal Joe noticed and called me into his office. He did not lecture or shame me. He simply said, gently, "Ian, you've made a small mistake here." My face went crimson. I braced for the reprimand I was sure was coming. Instead, he looked up and said, "It's no problem. We'll fix it before it goes home." That was it. No humiliation. No performance review. Just a gracious correction offered with dignity.

He taught me something I have carried for more than thirty years: correction does not have to wound, and guidance does not have to shame. Kindness teaches more effectively than criticism ever will. Thank you, Principal Joe.

There is a particular kind of strength in recovery. It signals resilience, humility, and the willingness to stay present when the moment is uncomfortable. People trust leaders who can rebound because it feels human. It feels honest. It feels safe.

What you dwell on grows. If you focus on missed notes, they become louder in your mind than they ever were in the room, but if you treat them as brief signals, small pieces of feedback, you free yourself to keep making the music that matters.

No great performance has ever been perfect. The same is true of leadership. Your impact is measured not by precision, but by consistency. Not by flawlessness, but by integrity. Not by what you miss, but by how you respond when you do.

Don't dwell on the missed notes. They are part of the music, but they are never the whole song.

CHAPTER 11:

Judge Your Work Without Judging Yourself

One of the quietest challenges in both music and leadership is learning how to evaluate your work without turning the evaluation into a verdict on who you are. Musicians face this constantly. You replay a piece in your mind or listen to a recording, and all you hear is what went wrong: the note that wobbled, the timing that slipped, the tone that wasn't what you imagined. It is easy for those imperfections to creep inward until you start to believe the problem is not the performance but the performer.

Leadership magnifies the temptation.

Every decision, every conversation, every moment of influence carries weight, and when something goes sideways, the reflex can be harsh self-judgment. You replay the meeting where you misspoke. You analyze the conversation where someone was left upset. You wonder why you didn't see the issue sooner or handle it differently. Before long, you are no longer evaluating the situation. You are evaluating yourself, and the judgment is rarely kind.

I learned the difference between judging the work and judging myself through a recording I made in my early days of playing guitar. I played a piece I had practiced for weeks, one I felt reasonably confident in. Later, listening back, I heard every flaw. One section rushed. Another dragged. A chord came out thin. A transition felt clumsy. I winced, stopped the recording, and considered deleting it, even though no one else would ever hear it.

But something made me listen again, this time not only for mistakes, but for progress. I noticed places where my timing had improved, parts where my tone was warmer than before, and a difficult shift that almost sounded effortless. Two truths were present at once: the recording was imperfect, yet better than anything I had played a month earlier.

That was the first time I understood how easily we underestimate growth by focusing only on friction.

Leadership requires the same lens adjustment. You must be able to see your work clearly, the parts that need refinement, and the parts that reflect real progress, without collapsing the entire evaluation into a story about your worth. If you make every misstep personal, you stop taking risks. You begin protecting your ego instead of serving your community. You play smaller, safer. The music suffers, and so do the people who depend on you.

Judging your work is a responsibility. Judging yourself is self-sabotage.

Leaders who endure learn to create a small internal space where honesty and self-compassion can coexist. They can say, "That conversation didn't go well," without adding, "because I am incompetent." They can say, "I should have handled that differently," without spiraling into shame. They see decisions as snapshots, not portraits. Work can be corrected, refined, and improved, while identity remains intact.

What surprised me, as I grew into leadership, was how much freedom lives in this distinction. When you stop tying your value to performance, you become more open to feedback. You listen more closely. You recover more quickly. You apologize without defensiveness. You take accountability without collapsing. People trust you more, not because you are perfect, but because you are stable.

Schools are full of moments that test this. A conversation with a teacher that feels heavier than it should. A decision you revisit and realize was not the right one. A meeting that drifts despite your best intentions. A student whose needs you did not recognize soon enough. In these moments, your inner voice matters. If it can be honest without being cruel, your leadership expands. If it only knows critique, your world becomes small.

I have come to think of leadership like a long practice session. Some days feel like breakthroughs. Some feel like setbacks. Most fall somewhere in between. None of them defines you. They shape you. They refine your tone. They teach you what works and what doesn't, but they do not decide your worth.

Judge your work because growth depends on it. Do not judge yourself, because worth does not depend on performance. That is dignity.

Hold that tension, and you will lead with more clarity, more courage, and far more generosity toward others and toward the person you are still becoming.

"You've got to learn to leave the table when love's no longer being served."

Quincy Jones

CHAPTER 12:
Loop Pedals: Hearing Yourself Honestly

The first time you step on a loop pedal and hear yourself played back, there is a jolt of recognition, equal parts fascination and discomfort. The loop doesn't lie. It repeats exactly what you just played, not what you meant to play, and not what you hoped would come out. Every hesitation, every rushed transition, every uneven strum returns with perfect accuracy. It is an intimate kind of feedback. You hear yourself as others would.

It can be unsettling. It can also be clarifying. The loop pedal offers an honest mirror.

Leaders rarely have loop pedals, yet they need them just as much. Leadership is full of moments when your impact and your intention drift apart in ways you do not recognize at the time. A gentle comment lands with unintended sharpness. A decision meant to provide consistency feels to others like rigidity. A silence you believed was respectful becomes interpreted as disinterest. You are always communicating, even when you are unaware of what message others are receiving.

I learned this early when a colleague approached me after a meeting I thought had gone well. "I know you didn't mean it this way," she said carefully, "but your tone came across as impatient." I was surprised and defensive at first because impatience was the furthest thing from my intention. But she wasn't describing what I meant. She was describing her experience. That distinction, once I let it in, changed everything.

Her feedback was a loop pedal moment. I heard myself from someone else's vantage point, and it revealed a truth I had been avoiding: leadership is not defined by what you mean. It is defined by what people feel.

The best leaders I have known create their own version of a loop pedal. They check their impact. They invite reflection. They ask for the truth, even when it is uncomfortable. They listen not to defend themselves, but to understand what others heard. Their goal is not to preserve the illusion of competence, but to refine the substance of their presence.

Of course, hearing yourself honestly is harder than it sounds. Most people avoid hearing their recorded voice. Hearing your recorded behavior is even harder. A loop pedal does not flatter you. It reveals you. But it also gives you a chance to adjust. You can slow down a rushed section, add warmth where the tone went thin, repair trust where something unintentionally cracked.

I once watched a student use a loop pedal, layering rhythm over rhythm, building a sound bigger than anything he had produced before. At one point, he laughed at a clumsy mistake looping behind him, but he didn't stop. He adjusted. He layered something smoother over the top. By the end, the loop he had been embarrassed by became part of the texture. The mistake didn't disappear. It simply stopped defining the sound.

Leadership evolves in the same way. Earlier loops, early tone, early missteps become part of your story, but not the whole of it. You grow by layering new awareness, new skills, and new presence over what used to embarrass you. Honest self-reflection is not about erasing what came before. It is about building something richer on top of it.

What matters most is your willingness to hear yourself clearly, not through the forgiving filter of your intentions, but through the honest resonance of your impact. When you understand how you land with others, your leadership becomes more aligned, more trustworthy, and more humane.

A loop pedal doesn't change who you are. It teaches you to hear yourself with enough honesty to grow.

“I worked on ‘Hallelujah’ for years.”

Leonard Cohen

CHAPTER 13:
Drafts, Dead Ends, and Doing It Again

Creatives eventually learn that most of what they produce will never reach the final stage. Songs begin as sketches. Melodies drift in and out before settling. Drafts get abandoned halfway through. Ideas that feel brilliant at midnight fall apart in the morning light. The process is full of false starts, wrong turns, and quiet disappointments.

Musicians live with this more comfortably than most people do. They know the song you hear on an album wasn't born complete. It was built from dozens of earlier versions, some chaotic, some promising, some painful, some forgettable. What remains is the version that survived the test of persistence.

Leadership has its own trail of drafts and dead ends.

I used to think effective leadership meant getting it right the first time. I imagined skilled leaders crafting perfect plans, making flawless decisions, and carrying out their work with seamless precision. The longer I stayed in school, the more I realized how messy the real process is. Leadership, like songwriting, unfolds through exploration. You try something, watch it wobble, adjust, try again, and only later understand which parts mattered.

There have been initiatives I believed in deeply that never found traction, committees that started with energy and dissolved under competing demands, conversations I approached at the wrong time or with the wrong tone, strategies I hoped would spark change but instead created confusion. These experiences used to trouble me more than they should have. I worried that abandoned ideas were evidence of weakness.

But drafts and dead ends are not failures. They are part of the creative rhythm of leadership.

One year, I wrote a song I loved in theory but could never quite finish. The chorus felt strong, but every verse weakened it. I tried different keys, tempos, and bridges. I rewrote each section again and again. Every attempt brought something new, but nothing fit. Eventually, I let it go, not because the idea was bad, but because I had not yet grown into it.

Months later, while working on an entirely different piece, parts of that abandoned song resurfaced. A line from one draft. A chord progression from another. A rhythmic idea I had discarded. What emerged wasn't the original song. It was something better, built from the best fragments of what hadn't worked.

Leadership often works the same way. An initiative that falters one year becomes the foundation of something stronger the next. A lesson learned from one misstep becomes the wisdom that steadies you later. A program that fails to take root may teach you something essential about timing, culture, or readiness. None of it is wasted. Every draft shapes the leader you are becoming.

What matters is your willingness to try again, to approach the same problem with a new lens, to accept that your first idea may not be the one that endures. Dead ends are simply places where the path needs refining, not proof that there is no path.

I once worked with a teacher who said, "I'm afraid to try this. What if it doesn't work?" I understood the fear, but we both knew that nothing meaningful emerges without risk. Drafts are risks. So are revisions. So are new attempts after disappointment. Leadership is not a performance of certainty. It is a commitment to keep shaping something worthwhile, even when early versions feel fragile.

With time, I came to appreciate the patience leadership demands. Not everything will land, not everything will last, but each attempt moves you closer to clarity. Each failed version teaches you something the successful version relies on. Each experience adds to the repertoire you draw from later.

Dead ends are not the end of the road. They are turns that didn't lead where you expected. The skill is not avoiding them. It is carrying their lessons forward.

The willingness to start again, to reimagine, rewrite, and rebuild is one of the most underappreciated strengths of good leadership. It keeps your work alive, adaptable, and honest.

The song you end up with is rarely the one you imagined at the start, but if you stay with the process, it often becomes something even better.

"Some nights you don't feel like playing. Those are the nights that define whether you are a performer."

Unattributed

CHAPTER 14:
Changing the Key Without Changing the Song

There is a simple tool that guitarists use, which can transform a piece of music: the capo. It is small and almost insignificant looking, but when clipped to the guitar's neck, the entire key of the song lifts. Familiar chord shapes suddenly sound brighter or lighter. The melody becomes easier to sing. The mood shifts. Yet, beneath the change, the song itself, its structure, its meaning, its identity, remains intact.

It took me years to understand how often leadership requires the same shift. You do not always rewrite the song; sometimes you adjust the key so that it can be played and heard more effectively in the moment.

Early in my career, I believed consistency meant sameness. I thought being steady required treating every situation the same way, speaking in the same tone, using the same strategies, and maintaining the same posture. I assumed predictability would make me trustworthy. What I did not yet understand was that people change, context changes, and the emotional temperature of a school shifts constantly. Leaders must be responsive enough to keep up.

You may be the same leader, but the key you play has to shift.

I remember a student who came into my office, overwhelmed by something that, at first glance, appeared small. My instinct was to respond with calm reassurance, but the moment I began to speak, I realized calm was not what he needed. He needed immediacy. Someone who could meet the intensity he was feeling, not mute it. So, I shifted. I raised my energy, leaned in, and matched the urgency of the moment. The support I offered did not change. The key did.

Leaders often cling to a single mode of communication because it feels safe or efficient, but people do not encounter leadership in neutral conditions. They arrive carrying fear, excitement, exhaustion, hope, confusion, defensiveness, and pride. Your ability to adjust tone without abandoning integrity becomes the bridge between you and them.

Changing the key is not changing yourself. It is not inauthentic. It is intentional.

A capo does not alter the song's structure. It moves the song into a range that fits the moment. Leadership does the same. You may deliver the same message but adjust the frame. You hold the same expectations but shift the tone. You maintain the same boundaries but change how you communicate them. Your values remain fixed, even as your approach adapts.

This balance, consistency of values paired with flexibility of delivery, is one of the hardest leadership skills to develop. Too much rigidity and you lose connection. Too much accommodation and you lose direction. The art lies in knowing when to shift the key so that what you are offering can actually be heard.

Schools test this constantly. A teacher motivated by direct feedback may feel crushed by the same tone that energizes someone else. A family in crisis may need more softness than structure. A student who has felt unseen may require a presence deeper than your default mode. The song remains yours, but the key must change if it is going to resonate with different listeners.

Some leaders mistake adaptation for inconsistency. Others mistake flexibility for weakness. Both misunderstandings limit impact. Leadership is not about proving you can play one song in one key forever. It is about ensuring the people you serve can hear the music you are trying to create.

The capo taught me what leadership eventually confirmed: you can shift without losing yourself. You can change the key without changing the song. Often, the shift is what makes the song its best.

People trust leaders who remain recognizable, rooted in values, anchored in integrity, and flexible enough to meet them where they are. That is real consistency. The kind that lasts.

"Inspiration is for amateurs. The rest of us just show up and get to work."

Jack White

CHAPTER 15:
Stop Waiting for Your Muse

There is a romantic image of creativity that many of us absorb long before we ever pick up an instrument or step into leadership. It is the myth of the muse, a mysterious force that arrives at exactly the right moment with clarity, energy, and inspiration. According to the myth, breakthrough comes first, and work follows.

Anyone who has spent time with musicians knows the truth. The muse is unreliable. She is beautiful, but inconsistent. She disappears for weeks. She shows up at inconvenient moments. If you wait for her, you will never create anything lasting.

What moves the work forward is far less glamorous. You sit down with your instrument when you do not feel ready, when the ideas feel stale, when the day has been long. You begin anyway. Slowly, sometimes imperceptibly, something takes shape. The work becomes the muse.

Leadership works the same way.

If you wait for the perfect moment, you will wait forever. If you wait to feel confident, energized, or fully prepared, the work will move on without you. Schools do not pause for inspiration. They shift. They surprise you. They ask you to show up even when you are tired, uncertain, or quietly wishing someone else would step in.

Some of the most meaningful leadership moments in my career happened on days when I did not feel particularly wise or grounded. A student knocked on my door, and I opened it despite the fatigue in my body. A teacher reached out in frustration, and I met with them without the perfect words. A parent called late in the day, and I listened, unsure that I could offer anything useful.

Leadership rarely rewards hesitation. It rewards presence.

You can wait for inspiration, but people need you now.
You can wait for clarity, but clarity often arrives only after you act.
You can wait to feel brave, but courage is almost always a decision, not a feeling.

There was a period when I delayed an initiative because I wanted the plan to be perfect. I waited for the right timing, the right energy, the right alignment. That moment never came. The work only moved forward when I accepted that I had to start imperfectly. Direction emerged after I began.

A muse did not bring clarity. The work did.

Children understand this instinctively. They draw because they want to draw. They practice until capability appears. Adults are the only ones who wait to feel ready before they begin.

In leadership, readiness is often discovered in retrospect. You realize you were more prepared than you thought because you allowed yourself to step in before certainty arrived.

Creativity in both music and leadership requires stubborn faithfulness. Showing up when inspiration is silent. When you sit with your guitar on days the music feels distant, you teach your hands consistency. When you step into leadership on days your confidence feels thin, you teach your voice steadiness.

The muse has her place. She brings color and spark, but she is not the engine. The work is.

The leaders who make the deepest impact are not the ones who wait. They act. They speak. They support. Their presence creates momentum. Their consistency creates trust. The muse eventually finds people who are already working.

So, stop waiting. Begin anyway. Most of what matters is created by people who do not feel ready but play anyway.

"They were feeling ripped off… Wouldn't you?"

Al Kooper

(On Bob Dylan at Newport)

CHAPTER 16:
When the Audience Boos

There is a particular kind of silence that settles over a performer the first time an audience reacts badly or does not react at all. It is not anger at first. It is disbelief. You are offering something you practiced, something you cared about, something you hoped would connect, and instead of applause, there is a murmur, a groan, a shake of the head, or in the worst moments, a boo.

Someone once told me that every new educational leader is perfect on the day they arrive, right up until they make their first decision.

Leadership has its own version of being booed, and it is far more personal.

You introduce an initiative you believe will help students, only to meet resistance behind closed doors. You make a decision, rooted in safety, and someone accuses you of overreacting. You speak plainly, and someone bristles. You offer feedback, and it is heard as an attack. You follow your values, and someone dislikes the sound of it.

The first time this happens, you question everything. Your judgment, your timing, your tone, your place in the work. You wonder if you misread the moment or should have chosen a different path. The exposure cuts deeply because leadership is not a performance of a song. It is a performance of yourself.

It took me years to realize that being booed is not always evidence of error. Sometimes it is evidence of necessity.

I once made a decision that protected a vulnerable child and frustrated adults who preferred convenience over discomfort. The backlash was immediate. Emails. Whispers. Tension in meetings. The instinct to retreat was powerful, but the decision was right. The child was safer because I held firm. The disagreement remained.

A mentor later told me, "If you lead long enough, someone will always be unhappy. Let their unhappiness sharpen your clarity, not your self-worth."

That sentence changed everything. Leadership is not a popularity contest. Disapproval is not always an indictment. Sometimes it means you are addressing what needs to be addressed.

Not all boos are unjustified. Some point to the tone you misjudged, the timing you mishandled, the context you overlooked. The challenge is learning to distinguish between resistance that signals misalignment and resistance that signals necessary disruption.

Being booed does not end the performance. It tests the foundation beneath you. It asks whether your conviction is rooted in ego or purpose. Whether you can remain steady without becoming defensive. Whether you can keep playing while being watched more critically than you would like.

Every seasoned leader remembers a moment they stayed upright while disapproval echoed from the balcony. Not because it felt good, but because it proved something about resilience. You survived. You returned. You showed up the next day without surrendering your integrity.

Musicians know one audience reaction does not define their work. Leaders must remember the same. Your sound is shaped over time, across countless decisions and conversations. One reaction does not erase an entire season of leadership.

When the audience boos, breathe.
Stay present.
Listen for what is true.
Release what is not.
Then keep playing.

The measure of leadership is not whether everyone likes your song. It is whether you are willing to keep playing, knowing some days bring applause and others bring boos.

INTERLUDE:
That One Concert Where Everything Went Wrong

If you're a musician, you probably have a story about a performance that unraveled beyond repair. A night when nothing cooperated: not the sound system, not the nerves, not the fingers that should have known better.

Mine happened while playing with my band, Lunchbox. It should have been forgettable. A low-stakes show in a small space with a small crowd. No pressure. No expectations. Which is probably why the mistakes felt so enormous. There was nowhere to hide.

Halfway through our first song, "Super Big Gulp," my mind went blank. Not a graceful pause, but an absolute void. I reached for a chord I had played a hundred times, and nothing came. My fingers stiffened. I glanced up, hoping no one noticed, and caught the eye of a man in the second row, whose expression told me everything.

He noticed.

I was fairly certain I could read his mind. "You suck," it said.

Then the technical issues began. When I hit the stomp box, the volume dropped. My voice caught on a chorus I usually sang without thinking. I broke a string and had to stop the set to replace it. The new string stayed out of tune for the rest of the night. By the middle of the set, it felt as though the evening had been carefully booby-trapped. Each mistake made the next one more likely. My hands were sweating. My timing unraveled. I knew exactly how badly it was going.

To cap it off, the payout at the end of the night was four dollars per band member.

Yes. Four dollars.

And yet, something unexpected happened. The room didn't fall apart. No one left. A few people smiled encouragingly. One person clapped early, as if applauding perseverance rather than performance. There was kindness in the room I had not anticipated. That kindness steadied me enough to keep going. We laughed, too, and that helped.

When the set ended, a man approached me and said, "You know, I really admired that you kept going. You didn't pretend it was perfect. You just stayed with it."

He meant it as a compliment. At the time, it felt like being praised for surviving a storm I had created myself. It took me years to understand what he was really saying.

Sometimes your worst performance teaches people more about you than your best one ever could.

Leadership is full of days like that. Moments when nothing goes as planned, when timing slips, when instincts misfire, when meetings derail, when conversations go wrong, when initiatives unravel despite preparation. Days when you feel exposed, human, and painfully imperfect.

These moments are not flattering, but they are formative.

These moments reveal your steadiness. They show whether you can remain present when embarrassed, grounded when rattled, and honest when you feel the pull to bluff your way through.

I look back on that disastrous show now with something close to fondness. Not because it went well (it did not), but because it taught me something applause never could: that continuing after faltering is its own kind of courage, that honesty is more compelling than polish, and that people forgive mistakes far more easily than they forgive inauthenticity.

Some performances, some meetings, some days, some seasons, will go wrong no matter how much you prepare. The question is never whether you can prevent every mistake; it is whether you can stay open, stay present, and stay yourself when the moment falls apart.

Everyone has that one concert where everything goes wrong.

The mistakes will not be what people remember; they will remember who you became in the middle of them.

PART III
Harmony and Working with Others

Teams, trust, conflict, culture

"When we sang together, something happened that didn't happen when we were apart."

Art Garfunkel

CHAPTER 17:
Harmony

Harmony Sounds Beautiful But Takes Practice.

Harmony is one of the quiet miracles of music. A single note can be clean and expressive. Add a second, then a third, and something larger appears. The sound becomes richer, deeper, and more textured than any one voice can be alone. Harmony is distinct parts choosing to belong to something shared.

It is also one of the hardest skills to master, because harmony requires more than talent. It requires awareness. You can play the right note at the wrong volume and ruin the blend. You can enter too early or too late, and it can pull the whole line off center. You can insist on your melody without listening, and collaboration turns into noise. Harmony is not only what you play. It is how you listen, how you adjust, how you make room for the larger sound.

Leadership, especially in schools, is the daily practice of harmony.

Early in my career, I assumed good leadership meant being the clearest voice in the room, the one who set direction and tempo. I thought my job was to lead from the front, steady and unshakable. Over time, I learned something less dramatic and far truer: much of leadership is blending. It is attuning to others, noticing the emotional pitch of a meeting, hearing what sits beneath a colleague's silence, recognizing when someone else's idea is the melody that needs to lead.

Schools are full of instruments: teachers with distinct styles, students with shifting rhythms, families with their own histories and expectations. Each brings a sound into the shared space. The strength of a school is rarely determined by the brilliance of one performer. It is determined by whether the voices learn to connect.

Harmony does not mean sameness. If every voice in a choir sang the same note, the sound would lose its depth. Harmony allows differences to become beauty. It welcomes variation, tension, and contrast. It says, "You don't have to match me, but you do have to listen. And I will listen to you." That discipline is where leadership matures.

I once worked with a leader who believed he was a visionary. He talked about a "master plan" he rarely shared and acted as though he were the conductor. He surrounded himself with friends and mirrored thinking. Instead of building harmony, he insisted on one loud note. Good people drifted away. A choir singing a single note is not music. It is noise.

That team taught me the real meaning of harmony: the willingness to let your sound enhance, not overpower, the people around you.

Harmony is also fragile. One tired day. One careless comment. One misunderstanding. One moment of unchecked ego. That is sometimes all it takes to tilt the balance. Leadership is noticing those shifts early and guiding people back toward connection before small dissonances harden into fractures.

The power of harmony is not the absence of conflict. It is the commitment to resolve it. Musicians do not eliminate tension. They use it. They let dissonance resolve into something honest. Leadership asks the same of us: not to avoid disagreement, but to shape it into something constructive and human.

In rehearsal, musicians pause, retune, and try again. Not because they failed, but because harmony requires tending. Leadership works the same way. You check your tone. You listen again. You lower your volume so someone else can rise. You bring your full self while leaving enough space for others to bring theirs.

Harmony is the sound of belonging. It is what happens when people choose to create something together rather than beside each other, and it is one of the most powerful gifts a leader can give a community: helping them to hear their collective music, especially on the days they forget they are a band at all.

"We always thought of ourselves as a band, not a backing group for one person."

Peter Buck (R.E.M.)

CHAPTER 18:
Keep the Band Together

Bands do not fall apart because the music stops. They fall apart because the space between the people making the music becomes strained. Talent rarely breaks a group; ego, misunderstanding, silence, and fatigue do. The small, unspoken fractures that grow in the shadows eventually shake the entire sound.

When you are young, you assume great bands succeed because every member is extraordinary, but anyone who has spent time inside a real ensemble knows the truth: great bands survive because someone, often quietly and without fanfare, keeps the band together.

That person listens differently. They notice tension before it erupts. They check in when someone starts drifting to the edges. They remind the group what they are building. They interpret tone and intention. They see beyond the performance into the relationships that make the performance possible.

Leadership is full of moments like this, moments when your most important job is not to push the work forward, but to hold the people together while they do it. That work is not sentimental. It is difficult. It runs against the pressure schools live under, the pressure to produce, to deliver, to keep moving. Outsiders often apply that pressure without understanding a basic truth: you cannot produce without the people. You cannot sustain outcomes without trust. Without harmony, you are just generating noise.

I learned this early as a school leader during a year when the workload was crushing, and the faculty felt stretched thin. The school was growing fast. Expectations were rising. Stress settled into the building like humidity. Meetings got shorter. Conversations got sharper. Patience thinned. Every small disagreement felt amplified. It was not that people stopped caring. They were exhausted.

And I pushed on.

I drove forward because I thought that was what leadership required. Results had to come. People would "get it done." And they did, because they were good and because they cared. But they were doing it on hot coals and razor blades, and I did not yet have the maturity to see what that was costing.

In hindsight, the real work was not structural. It was relational. The team did not need another initiative or a more polished plan. They needed a connection. They needed someone to steady the rhythm section so the melody could breathe again. They needed clarity about what mattered most, and permission to stop pretending everything was fine.

I should have slowed things down, not pushed them forward at all costs.

Not with a lecture. Not with forced positivity. Not by trying to orchestrate harmony through slogans. By re-centering attention on the people behind the work. By checking in with people one-on-one, not to "solve" them, but to understand them. By naming what was happening out loud, so that it did not keep leaking into everything else. By cutting nonessential items, to allow the team to recover capacity. By building small moments of rest and laughter into meetings, because fatigue does not respond to urgency. By making space for honest conversations before silence turned into something harder to repair.

The music might not have improved instantly, but the tone would have had a chance to change, and slowly, the band could have re-formed and come back to itself.

Keeping the band together does not mean eliminating conflict. Musicians argue. Staff teams disagree. Creative people clash. Strong educators have strong opinions. However, when trust is strong and relationships are tended, conflict becomes a form of creativity rather than a source of rupture.

Some leaders convince themselves that disconnection is inevitable, that teams drift apart over time, no matter what you do. But disconnection is rarely random. It grows when leaders stop watching the emotional edges, when they focus on outcomes more than relationships, when they treat people like instruments rather than musicians, when they assume harmony is self-sustaining rather than something that needs tuning.

Keeping the band together requires humility. You must step back sometimes, so that others can step forward. You must let someone else's idea lead. Be willing to admit mistakes, accept misunderstandings, and apologize promptly. It is not glamorous work. No one applauds the leader who prevents the fracture that never becomes public, but communities survive because of this quiet labor.

The best leaders I have known were not the flashiest. They were the ones who kept the band together through seasons of strain. They did not panic at the first sign of tension. They did not micromanage. They did not reshuffle the setlist every time someone hit a sour note. They paid attention. They protected the relationships that protected the work.

There is a moment in every band, every school, every team, when someone feels like walking away. They feel unheard, tired, undervalued, or confused about direction. Keeping the band together does not mean forcing anyone to stay. It means making it unmistakably clear that they matter, that their voice counts, and that the music is richer with them in it.

When people feel that, they stay, not out of obligation, but out of belonging, and belonging is the heartbeat of any ensemble. It is the thread that keeps the music alive.

CHAPTER 19:
Know Your Audience

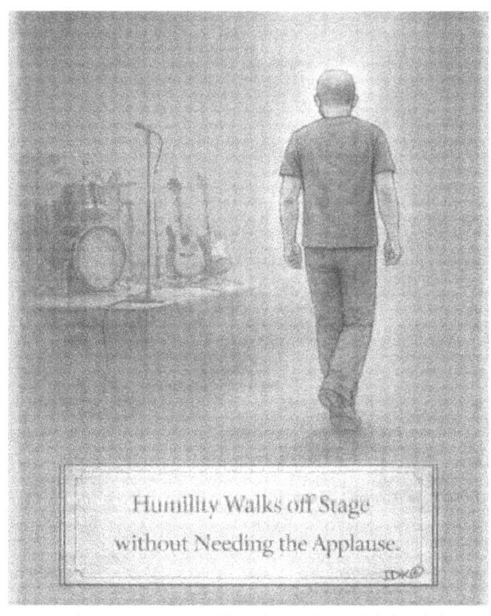

The audience changes everything. You can rehearse a song until it feels effortless in an empty room, but the moment you step onstage, the room itself becomes part of the performance, and so do the people in it. Energy shifts. Silence carries weight. Restlessness pulls at the rhythm. You adjust instinctively, not by abandoning the song, but by responding to what the room gives you and what it withholds.

Knowing your audience is not about pandering. It is about awareness.

Musicians do not play to an audience; they play with one. They listen as much as they perform. They sense when to press forward and when to ease back. They recognize when the room is ready for intensity and when it needs restraint. The audience is not an obstacle to overcome; it is a partner in the exchange.

Leadership works the same way.

In schools, every room carries its own emotional climate. A faculty meeting after a long week is not the same room as a faculty meeting after a crisis. A parent gathering during uncertainty requires a different tone than one held in celebration. A classroom full of students arrives with stories already in motion before you ever speak. A colleague seeking clarity needs something different from a colleague seeking reassurance.

Leaders who fail to read the room often deliver the right message in the wrong moment, and the moment almost always wins.

I learned this during a meeting that should have been straightforward. The agenda was clear. The purpose was reasonable. I walked in ready to share updates and move us forward, but the instant I entered the room, something felt off. The teachers were quiet, not focused quiet, but heavy quiet. The kind that carries fatigue.

I noticed it.
And ignored it.

I pressed ahead with the tone I had prepared, and the room resisted everything I said without meaning to. They were not disagreeing. They simply could not receive what I was offering. My words landed flat, not because they were wrong, but because they were mistimed.

Halfway through, I stopped. I named what I was seeing. I asked what was going on.

A few people exhaled, and the truth surfaced. It was the one-year anniversary of the death of a fourth-grade teacher. I had not forgotten the date, but I had underestimated its weight. The room did not need efficiency or momentum. It needed acknowledgment. It needed humanity.

That day taught me something essential: leadership is not only about what you say.
It is about whether your tone recognizes the emotional truth of the people in front of you.

You cannot rush a tired audience.
You cannot hype a grieving one.
You cannot push a fearful room, and you cannot lecture a confused one.

You also cannot avoid the truth people need.
You simply have to deliver it in the key they can hear.

Knowing your audience is an act of respect. It says: I see you as you are, not as I wish you to be.

When performers talk about "winning a room," they do not mean manipulating it. They mean joining it. They mean stepping into the emotional landscape with enough awareness to adjust without abandoning themselves. Leadership asks the same. You listen before you speak. You sense the room before shaping it. You adjust your volume, pacing, and posture while staying anchored in your values.

There are moments, of course, when the audience is resistant even when you read them well. Not hostile, just not ready. The timing is wrong. The emotional window is narrow. In those moments, knowing your audience also means knowing when to wait. Not to surrender the message, but to choose a moment when it can land with care rather than force.

Patience is not avoidance.
It is discernment.

The more consistently you read the room, the more people will trust you. They begin to feel understood before you ever speak. They sense that you are paying attention, not performing leadership, but practicing it. That trust becomes the foundation for every hard conversation, every cultural shift, every moment that requires courage on both sides.

Musicians know when an audience is with them. They feel it in the stillness between notes, in the way silence deepens instead of disperses, in the warmth that gathers rather than evaporates. Leaders feel it too. They feel the room lean in. They feel people breathe together. They feel the moment open.

When you know your audience, you stop just leading people and start leading with them.

That is when leadership finds its fullest tone, not when your voice is the loudest in the room, but when it is the one the room trusts enough to follow.

CHAPTER 20:
The Gig Starts Before You Walk In

Musicians learn quickly that the posted start time of a show is not when the gig actually begins. The gig starts long before the first chord rings out, long before the audience arrives, long before the lights come up. It begins in preparation no one sees. Tuning instruments. Adjusting levels. Testing microphones. Walking the room to understand how it will hold sound.

The most reliable musicians are not the ones who dazzle onstage. They are the ones who arrive ready.

Leadership is no different.

In schools, the "gig" rarely starts when the meeting is scheduled, the bell rings, or the parent steps into your office. It begins earlier, in the breath you take to steady yourself before you enter, in the quick scan of the emotional climate before you speak, in the choice to bring calm into a tense room.

Being early in leadership is not about punctuality. It is about readiness.

I misunderstood this early in my career. I believed that if I showed up at the right time with the right information, the rest would fall into place. Almost always, the moments that went wrong were the ones I entered hurriedly. I carried tension from one conversation into the next. I let urgency eclipse humanity.

I remember walking into a teacher meeting during an intense season. Just minutes before, I had finished a parent conversation that ended with a threat of legal action. I was technically on time, but I arrived late, late in tone, late in presence. A teacher in that meeting was vulnerable, carrying more than most of us knew. Had I paused for even ten seconds outside the door, had I begun the gig before stepping inside, I would have led differently. More gently. More fully.

That moment changed me. It taught me that leadership is not measured by arrival time. It is measured by the readiness you bring when you arrive.

Musicians know that if you rush soundcheck or skip tuning, the entire performance suffers. A late adjustment does not just inconvenience the band; it disrupts the sound. Leadership carries the same responsibility. When you show up unprepared, emotionally, relationally, mentally, the room shifts, and people feel it.

This is why the best leaders develop small soundchecks for themselves. Not dramatic rituals. Simple practices.

A pause at the door.
One steady breath in the hallway.
A quiet question: What does this room need from me right now?

Sometimes the room needs clarity. Sometimes containment. Sometimes warmth. Sometimes restraint. Readiness is the ability to adjust your internal settings before you ask others to adjust theirs.

Over time, I built my own rhythm. Some mornings I walked the campus before teachers arrived. I read bulletin boards. I noticed small changes. I felt the pace of the day before it accelerated. Those walks were not administrative tasks. They were grounding. They reminded me why I chose leadership in the first place.

But readiness is not only personal. It is also communal.

I once heard a story about a young band invited to open on a major tour. Instead of rushing them through a perfunctory check, the headlining band gave them real time to soundcheck. The gesture was not logistical; it was dignifying. It said, your sound matters. Take the time to get it right. That young band was Rush. The generous band was Kiss.

Years later, Rush would become one of the most technically disciplined bands in rock history. But before the discipline was public, it was protected.

Great leaders do the same. They shape the stage before the performance begins.

When you give a colleague a moment to gather themselves before a difficult conversation, you are starting the gig. When you protect a team from unnecessary overload so they can focus on essential work, you are starting the gig. When you enter a room with steadiness that calms rather than inflames, you are starting the gig.

Readiness does not require perfection. It requires intention. Presence instead of momentum. Responsiveness instead of reflex.

Schools move fast. The pace can be relentless. Within that speed, the leaders people trust are the ones who understand that leadership begins a few breaths before the moment everyone else thinks it does.

You pause.
You gather yourself.
You choose your tone.

The gig does not start when the room sees you.
It starts when you decide how you will show up in it.

"I think the reason why my fans connect with me is that I've always been honest with them."

Taylor Swift

CHAPTER 21:
Build Your Fanbase

In music, the word fanbase often conjures images of crowds, applause, and people chanting a name. Musicians know better. A real fanbase is not built through spectacle. It grows through consistency. The fans who stay are not the ones who are dazzled; they are the ones who trust you. They recognize your voice. They believe you will show up.

But trust alone is not enough. They stay because something in your music names something in them. They hear their own questions, longings, or convictions echoed back with clarity. Over time, a quiet mutuality forms. You show up with honesty and craft; they show up with attention and loyalty. The relationship is not fueled by hype but by recognition. They feel steadied rather than impressed, understood rather than entertained.

Leadership requires the same kind of following, though we rarely use the word. In schools, you do not need applause. You need trust. You need people who feel safe approaching you, who believe your presence reduces uncertainty rather than amplifying it, who know your words carry weight because your behavior consistently supports them.

Trust is your fanbase, and it is built slowly.

Early in my leadership, I assumed trust came from competence. Clear decisions. Confident communication. Strong performance. If I am honest, I also believed position mattered, that titles carried authority which naturally translated into trust. Experience corrected me. Competence may open the door, but it does not build a following. People can respect your skill and keep their distance.

Trust forms through consistency, through small, repeatable behaviors that reveal who you are over time.

A teacher once said to me, "I don't always agree with you, but I always know where you're coming from." At first, I did not know how to receive that. Later, I came to understand it as one of the deepest compliments a leader can earn. Agreement is optional. Trust is not.

The leaders I admired most were not the ones who won every argument or dominated every room. They were the ones who showed up reliably over time. Not predictably in personality, but dependable in principle. They listened carefully. They adjusted when the moment required it. They spoke plainly. They did not disappear when things became uncomfortable. They kept their commitments, especially the small ones. A leadership fanbase is simply the group of people who believe in your integrity.

They come to you when something is wrong because they trust you will not dismiss them. They ask for help because they believe you will handle their vulnerability with dignity. They follow your lead not because of your title, but because your tone has earned their confidence.

This cannot be manufactured. People read tone more clearly than language. They know when a leader is performing and when one is present. Once they sense authenticity, they lean in, not because they are persuaded, but because they feel safe.

I remember a moment that reshaped my understanding of this. A student approached me after school and said, "I don't really know you well, but I know you're safe." He did not mean physically safe, though that mattered. He meant emotionally reliable. Predictable in the right ways.

He was carrying something he had not yet put into words. There had been tension in his world, conflict, confusion, the kind of uncertainty that makes a young person scan for steadiness before they speak. He was not looking for a rescuer. He was looking for a place where his words would not be mishandled.

He had been watching, not intentionally, but in the quiet, perceptive way young people do. How I moved through the building. How I spoke to teachers. How I responded to frustration. How I greeted students in passing. Whether my tone shifted under pressure. Trust had been forming long before he ever needed it.

That afternoon, what he needed most was not brilliance or authority. He needed containment. He needed to know that if he said something difficult, I would not flinch, escalate, minimize, or disappear. Safety, in that moment, meant steadiness.

This is how leadership fanbases form: in the peripheral vision of those you serve. People notice how you speak about others when they are not in the room. How do you recover when you are wrong? How do you hold boundaries without losing kindness? They notice your steadiness long before they ever name it.

Titles may shine a light on you, but they do not keep people listening. Tone does.

When leaders change direction, new roles, new strategies, new contexts, people do not evaluate the shift by its novelty. They evaluate it by its integrity. If they believe the change is rooted in purpose rather than performance, they stay. If they sense approval-seeking, they drift.

Your credibility is not tied only to the song you are playing right now, but to the honesty with which you move through your set.

In music, artists keep their fanbase by staying true to their voice. In leadership, the same principle applies. You show up consistently. You keep your word. You listen deeply. You let people experience your humanity behind the title.

Applause fades. Trust remains.

CHAPTER 22:
The Bass Player Is Not a Backup

If you watch a band long enough, you learn that the loudest instrument rarely holds the music together. The melody gets attention. The solo earns applause. The singer draws the crowd. But the bass is what anchors the sound. It fills the spaces others overlook. It locks the rhythm in place. When the bass is missing, you feel it immediately, even if you cannot explain why.

The bass player is not backup.
The bass player is the foundation.

Great bass players understand this. Their work is not about flash. It is about presence. About holding the groove so others can take risks. About serving the song rather than standing in front of it. Leadership works the same way.

The most effective leaders are rarely the loudest. They are the ones who create stability. They listen deeply. They follow through. They keep the system in time so others can lead boldly.

Schools depend on this kind of leadership more than they realize.

Much of what sustains a school, the routines, the consistency, the emotional steadiness, the quiet problem-solving, comes from people whose work does not generate applause. Their contributions do not make headlines. They simply keep the place standing.

I learned this during a year of significant change. New initiatives. New pressures. New expectations. At times, the energy felt scattered, as if every department was improvising in a different key. Amid the noise, one colleague provided a steady bass line. She was not loud. She did not dominate meetings. She followed through. She anticipated problems. She checked in quietly. She shaped the culture without ever announcing it.

At first, I underestimated her influence. Her steadiness felt admirable but unremarkable until the day she was absent. Meetings drifted. Small miscommunications multiplied. Nothing collapsed, but the building lost its center of gravity.

That day clarified something essential: leadership does not only come from melody or harmony. Some leadership comes from bass, from reliability, presence, and the unglamorous work of holding things together.

Leaders make a mistake when they treat this as lesser work. They fail communities when they overlook the people who make others' success possible. The myth that leadership requires constant visibility is just that, a myth. Some of the most important leadership is nearly invisible because it is done so well.

Bass-line leadership requires humility. A willingness to serve without recognition. A commitment to the groove rather than the spotlight. There is strength in this role, the strength of someone who understands that excellence does not require center stage.

When I look back at the strongest teams of which I have been part, there was always someone playing bass. Someone who stabilized the rhythm. Someone who made it possible for others to soar because they kept the ground steady for landing.

When I feel myself drifting toward ego or frustration, I think of the bass. It reminds me that leadership is not about being noticed. It is about being essential.

The bass player is not a backup.
They are the pulse.

"It's not about being famous. It's about doing what you love."

Darlene Love

A key vocalist behind producer Phil Spector's signature layered sound, often singing on tracks that were credited to other groups. Inducted into the Rock and Roll Hall of Fame in 2011.

•

CHAPTER 23:
Sing Backup Sometimes

There is a quiet beauty in singing backup. Most people never notice it unless it is missing. They hear the melody first, the voice out front carrying the emotional weight of the song. Beneath that melody, though, are harmonies that lift, steady, and enrich the sound. Backup singers do not compete with the melody. They make it stronger.

This is one of the most underestimated skills in leadership.

Supporting roles carry dignity. Those who sing backup understand that contribution is not diminished by position. Their presence shapes the whole. They hold the line. They thicken the sound. They serve something larger than themselves.

Great leaders understand this instinctively.

Some moments require a clear lead. Others require support. Knowing the difference is wisdom.

In cultures that reward visibility, this instinct can feel countercultural. We often mistake leadership for presence and influence for airtime. But anyone who has spent time in schools knows the truth runs quieter. Some of the most stabilizing leaders are not the ones who dominate conversations, but the ones who make space for others to step forward, especially those whose voices are thoughtful, hesitant, or still forming.

I saw this clearly during a student leadership experience abroad. One student, confident, articulate, naturally took the lead. His voice became the melody. As the work unfolded, another student, quieter, more observant, offered an insight that shifted the conversation's direction. The first student paused. He recognized the moment. Instead of reclaiming the lead, he adjusted. He supported. He amplified.

The work that emerged was stronger than either voice alone.

That moment stayed with me because it captured something essential: leadership is not weakened by stepping back. It is strengthened.

Singing backup requires awareness, recognizing when another voice carries the truth of the moment. It requires humility, choosing contribution over credit. It requires confidence, trusting that influence does not disappear simply because you are not the loudest voice in the room.

Many leaders struggle here, especially those whose strengths lie in clarity, decisiveness, or verbal fluency. It can feel risky to soften your volume. But leadership is not a solo. It is an arrangement. Good arrangements depend on contrast, restraint, and listening.

Once I understood this, my leadership changed. Meetings became less about directing and more about amplifying. Conversations shifted from providing answers to drawing them out. I stopped assuming that leadership meant leading every moment.

Schools are full of emerging voices, teachers discovering their strengths, students finding confidence, colleagues growing into influence. When leaders insist on carrying every melody, the room shrinks. When leaders know how to sing backup, the room expands.

There is also a quieter truth here, one we do not often name: not everyone wants to sing lead all the time. Some people contribute best through reflection, preparation, and steadiness rather than immediacy. When leaders recognize and honor this, teams become more balanced, more humane, and more sustainable.

Backup singing also protects against burnout. You cannot carry every melody without exhaustion. When leadership is shared, capacity grows. Dependency fades. A culture of contribution replaces a culture of performance.

What I love most about singing backup is that it remains faithful to the music without needing you to carry the music alone. It lifts others without disappearing.

There are moments when leadership requires you to step forward clearly and decisively. There are just as many when your greatest impact comes from supporting someone else's lead.

Leadership is not measured by how often you sing the melody. It is measured by how well the song comes together.

Sometimes, the truest form of leadership is knowing when to listen closely, soften your volume, and add your voice only where it strengthens the whole.

"Even the hard times are part of your life story. If you acknowledge them and move past them, they eventually add up to the experience that makes you wise."

Miley Cyrus

CHAPTER 24:
When Bandmates Clash

Every band, no matter how talented or tightly knit, eventually reaches a moment when the music falters. Sometimes the conflict is small: a disagreement over tempo, a missed cue, a note played too loudly. Sometimes it is larger: a clash of personalities, a dispute about direction, an unspoken frustration finally surfacing. The songs do not stop, at least not at first, but the air changes. The harmony holds, but barely.

Leadership teams experience the same shift. The work continues, but something essential goes out of tune.

Few artistic conflicts illustrate the cost of fractured leadership more clearly than the split between Pink Floyd's bassist, Roger Waters, and guitarist, David Gilmour. For years, their creative tension produced music that reshaped rock history. Waters was the conceptual architect; Gilmour was the melodic heart. Together, they created work neither could have made alone.

Over time, that balance eroded. As Waters' vision grew more controlling, the collaborative space that sustained the band narrowed. Gilmour pushed back, quietly but firmly. What began as creative friction hardened into a struggle over ownership, identity, and control. Eventually, Waters left and attempted to prevent the band from continuing without him.

The courts disagreed. Pink Floyd, they ruled, was not the product of a single genius but of collective authorship. The band continued. Waters carried on independently, with conviction but a narrower reach.

This story is not about who was right. It is about what happens when leadership stops being shared.

When one voice dominates to the point that others no longer recognize themselves in the work, even extraordinary teams fracture. Brilliance becomes brittle when it is no longer built together.

Conflict, however, does not always end in rupture.

Fleetwood Mac offers a counterpoint. In the mid-1970s, the band was unraveling under the weight of personal loss, betrayal, jealousy, and exhaustion. By every rational measure, they should have collapsed. Instead, they stayed long enough to finish the work, tense, wounded, but present, and transformed their turmoil into music.

The result was *Rumors*, one of the best-selling albums in history. It was not created through emotional harmony, but through discipline, honesty, and respect for one another's craft, even when trust was strained.

The fractures did not disappear. In time, the band separated, pursued other paths, and carried the cost of what had happened. But years later, they reunited with clearer boundaries and greater maturity. Their history was not erased; it was integrated. The reunion was not nostalgia; it was evidence of growth.

Fleetwood Mac's story shows that when teams choose reflection over resentment, conflict need not be terminal. It can become material. And sometimes, with enough time and accountability, though broken alignment can be returned.

Leadership teams reveal the same patterns.

You can feel when a team slips out of sync. Conversations tighten. Humor thins. Meetings feel performative rather than generative. The work begins with struggling through what remains unspoken. Leaders often sense the imbalance long before it is named, but sensing is not the same as responding.

I remember a year when two colleagues, both excellent teachers and deeply committed to students, began to slide into quiet friction. It appeared in clipped emails, avoided eye contact, and kept conversations brief. I hoped it would pass. Tension rarely does.

They shared students. Their misalignment began affecting others.

After a meeting thick with discomfort, I asked them to meet, not for correction or mediation, but for conversation. Predictably, both minimized it.

"I'm fine."
"Just tired."

Exhaustion was not the cause. It was the amplifier.

Beneath the surface, each had constructed a story about the other. A misunderstanding became narrative. Narrative became distance. Distance hardened into defensiveness. When those stories were finally spoken aloud, the truth was disarmingly human: one felt unheard, the other misunderstood. Both cared deeply. That mattered.

The shift was not immediate or dramatic, but it was real. Their relationship did not return to what it had been. It became better, clearer, more professional, and more honest. They learned the difference between hearing and listening, between tension that signals growth and tension that signals warning.

Teams that endure understand something essential: conflict is not the opposite of harmony; it is how harmony is maintained. Left unaddressed, resentment festers. When conversation is avoided, small cracks widen into fractures. Without repair, teams drift apart while still standing side by side.

Harmonizing means recognizing when the music sounds strained and having the courage to stop and retune. It means treating conflict not as failure, but as information. It means believing people are more than their sharp edges, more than their worst moments or tired days.

The strongest teams are not those without conflict. They are those where people trust one another enough to work through it. Every band clashes. Every school does too. What matters is not whether conflict occurs, but whether leaders create conditions where people can return to one another with dignity.

Harmony is not the sound of perfect agreement. It is the sound of different voices choosing, again and again, to remain in the song together.

INTERLUDE:
Hallway Duty as Stage Presence

If you spend enough years in schools, you begin to realize that hallway duty is one of the most revealing places to understand leadership. Not the office. Not the meeting room. Not the stage at assemblies.

The hallway.

There is something about standing in that in-between space, between classes, between moods, between the private world a student brings from home and the public world of the school day, that exposes the truth of your presence. Students read you instantly. They read your energy, your expression, your posture. They know whether you are there or merely stationed. They sense whether you are open, distracted, tired, or genuinely glad to see them.

Hallway duty, in a strange way, is stage presence.

You are not performing, not exactly. You are showing up. Showing up well requires intention. The same way a musician steps into the light aware of the room, the tone, and the energy they carry, you step into the hallway knowing your presence shapes the climate around you.

I learned this more deeply than I expected. There were mornings when I entered the hallway carrying weight I had not shaken from the day before, a late-night email, a lingering conflict, a decision still turning in my mind. I thought I could hide it. I never could. Students passed with quick glances that seemed to ask, You, okay? They did not say it aloud. They did not need to.

They felt the shift.

There were other mornings, days when I felt grounded, open, when the hallway itself seemed to breathe differently. Students lingered. They joked. They approached. They let me into their world with an ease that could not be manufactured. The melody of the day began right there, on that stretch of tile, before any lesson or meeting had a chance to shape it.

What surprised me most was how much power lived in the smallest moments. A nod. A smile. A "good morning" that sounded like you meant it. A brief comment to a student you knew had a hard week. A simple acknowledgment that said, I see you.

These were not grand gestures.
They were not speeches.
They were not formal interventions.

They were the leadership equivalent of tuning your instrument before the song begins, small, precise adjustments that set the tone for everything that follows.

For years, I struggled to convey this to some teachers. I tried to explain that hallway duty was not about supervision or compliance. It was about connection. Stepping into the rhythm of the school day alongside students. Letting your presence register not as authority, but as steadiness.

Some understood immediately. Others treated hallway duty as something to endure rather than an opportunity to engage.

What I wanted them to see was this: those few minutes between bells are where trust quietly forms, where relationships breathe, where a simple greeting can soften a hard morning or offer acknowledgement to a child who may rarely feel seen. Being visible with students is not extra. It is foundational.

I think about hallway duty now as a metaphor for the everyday visibility of leadership. You do not get to choose when people are watching. You do not get to curate which moments reveal you.

The spaces between tasks, between decisions, between the "important" things, those are the moments when students and colleagues learn who you are.

They see you in passing, and those passing moments become the atmosphere they walk through.

Hallway duty is not glamorous, but it is honest, and honesty is where leadership becomes real.

PART IV: PERFORMANCE AND VISIBILITY

Courage, front-facing leadership, presence

CHAPTER 25:
Play Like You Are at Carnegie.

Musicians speak of Carnegie Hall with reverence. It is more than a venue; it is a symbol. The acoustics are unforgiving. The audience listens closely. The gravity of that stage demands your best. When you play at Carnegie, you do not wander in casually. You prepare. You breathe differently. You hold the instrument like it matters. You honor the moment because you understand its weight.

Seasoned performers learn something counterintuitive: you do not wait until you reach Carnegie to play like you are there.

You practice with that seriousness in rehearsal rooms. You bring that intention to tiny stages. Even when only a handful of people are listening, you shape your sound as if the space deserves your full presence. The stage does not make the musician. The musician makes the stage.

Leadership requires the same kind of presence.

You may never stand in front of thousands. You may never hold roles with spotlights or headlines. The moments you do step into, however small, meetings, morning greetings, difficult conversations, quiet decisions, deserve the same intention you would bring to the most visible moments of your career.

I remember the first time I saw a teacher embody this truth. It was an ordinary Tuesday morning. She stood in her doorway, greeting students as if she were welcoming honored guests into a carefully prepared space. Her voice was soft but steady. Her attention was undivided. Every student who crossed the threshold received something personal: a look, a word, an acknowledgment that said, you belong here.

It was not performance. It was presence.

Her classroom was her Carnegie.

Watching her changed me. It showed me that leadership quality is not defined by the size of your stage, but by the seriousness with which you treat the moments entrusted to you.

Leadership has dozens of hidden Carnegie Halls: the five-minute conversation with a teacher who is quietly unraveling, the meeting where one sentence sets the tone for the entire year, the day a student finally gathers the courage to tell you something difficult, the moment you choose to speak up when the room grows silent, the split-second decision that keeps someone safe.

These are your stages.

The people standing before you in those spaces, students, colleagues, families, deserve a presence that respects the weight of those moments.

Playing like you are at Carnegie does not mean being dramatic or flawless. It means bringing intentionality to ordinary settings. It means recognizing that what feels small to you may be monumental to someone else. It means understanding that your tone, your steadiness, your attention, these are instruments. How you use them shapes the emotional acoustics of every room you enter.

There have been times when I underestimated the impact of a moment: a quick hallway exchange I assumed would be forgotten, only to learn later that it stayed with a student for weeks. There have also been times I carried responsibility for harm: a careless remark, a tone that wounded, a dismissal that lingered. A short conversation with a teacher can shape their confidence more than we realize. A decision made quietly can change the trajectory of a child's school experience.

We do not always know when we are standing on a Carnegie stage. So, we learn to treat every moment with care, even when we are unsure of its significance.

The best leaders I know seem to carry this mindset naturally. They do not save their best tone for formal settings. They bring it everywhere. They show up fully, whether there are two people in the room or two hundred. They understand that leadership is not a performance. It is a presence. It is the steady commitment to bring intention, not perfection, to the work before you.

Playing like you are at Carnegie is not about pressure. It is about respect. It is about honoring the lives that intersect with yours each day. It is believed that every room, no matter how small, deserves your best sound.

In leadership, as in music, your best sound is not the loudest. It is the truest.

"You have to learn how to get along."

Dave Grohl

CHAPTER 26:
Clarity Over Comfort

No matter how many times you have performed, you know this moment all too well: the breath before stepping onto the stage, when the lights warm overhead, the monitors hum to life, and the quiet becomes almost physical, thick enough to feel on your skin. Backstage, the air carries dust, metal, and cable insulation. The guitarist beside you adjusts their strap one more time. The drummer taps a nervous rhythm on their thigh. Even if you have rehearsed flawlessly, even if you love the music, there is always that flicker of doubt, a tightening in the chest, a whisper: What if I'm not ready?

You hear your name. The stage manager nods.
You inhale.
You step forward.

You face the music.

Leadership has its own version of this moment, less theatrical, but just as exposing.

It happens when a difficult truth needs to be spoken and you know someone will resist it.
It happens when a necessary decision will disappoint people you admire.
It happens when you enter a room carrying a conflict that cannot be avoided.
It happens most intensely when a child's safety is at stake, and clarity is required, even as others hesitate.

These moments do not wait for emotional readiness. They arrive like stage cues.

The instinct to pause, to wait for more courage, more consensus, more approval, is deeply human, but leadership is not built within moments when everything feels in tune. It is forged in moments of dissonance, when truth, handled with care, is better than silence.

Every school year, I have felt those butterflies on opening day. Every difficult meeting came with a twist in the stomach. I wanted to get it right. I cared about the people in front of me. I respected their time and their craft and did not want to waste either.

I knew, as every leader eventually learns, that there would always be a percentage of people I would never fully reach, the ones in the back row, arms crossed, scanning for weakness, waiting for confirmation that I did not mean what I said.

I remember the first time I had to deliver news I knew would frustrate teachers. It wasn't dramatic, just necessary and hard. The decision protected students but disrupted routine. I rehearsed every word, checked details, and practiced tone. Still, walking into the room, the whisper returned: Are you sure you want to be the one to say this?

Leadership does not wait for emotional certainty.
It moves with moral clarity.

As I spoke, I felt the reactions ripple, surprise, frustration, resignation, quiet understanding. I began with, "This is hard for me to share, because I know it will impact everyone here." No one applauded, no one thanked me, but afterward, a teacher quietly said, "I didn't like the message, but I respected how you delivered it."

That sentence made me think.

Facing the music is not about being fearless. It is about being faithful to purpose, to students, to truth, to integrity.

Musicians understand that the audience does not need perfection; they need presence. Leadership echoes that truth. People do not need leaders who pretend to be unshakable. They need leaders who are honest, grounded, and willing to hold the hard moment without flinching, blaming, or disappearing.

The knot in your stomach before a difficult conversation is not weakness. It is a signal.

Neuroscience tells us that anticipatory anxiety is rarely about the event itself; it is about the possibility of being dismissed, misread, or judged. For leaders, that same biological spark can be reframed: This matters. This conversation carries weight. I care.

Over time, seasoned leaders become less afraid of discomfort and more curious about it. They learn to read it not as a warning sign, but as a compass.

There is a kind of false bravery in leadership, loud, performative, brittle. It storms into rooms with a puffed chest, projecting confidence while leaking insecurity at the edges. False bravery is armor. It protects ego, not community.

True bravery is quieter. Measured. Steady. It says, I don't have all the answers, but I have enough courage to speak the truth.

People feel the difference immediately.

There was a time when a teacher's behavior crossed a boundary that threatened a student's emotional safety, not a scandal, but a damaging pattern. Sitting across from that teacher, heart beating too fast, I knew that naming the issue might bruise pride but not naming it could harm a child.

I chose the child.

The conversation was firm, clear, and compassionate. The teacher bristled, then softened, then listened. Weeks later, they thanked me, not for the correction, but for the dignity with which it was delivered.

That moment taught me something essential: facing the music, when done with clarity and care, can strengthen relationships rather than fracture them.

There have also been times when I waited too long.

I once avoided addressing a conflict between two staff members, hoping tension would resolve itself. It didn't. It hardened. By the time I intervened, trust had eroded, and people had chosen sides. Repair was still possible, but it cost far more than it should have. The impact reverberated through the staff like the lingering resonance of a massive gong: the sound wasn't just heard; it was felt.

Silence is not neutral.
It amplifies what we fear to name.
Problems grow in the dark.

Every time I waited too long, I learned the same lesson: delay damages trust faster than the difficult truth.

Musicians miss notes, it's inevitable. The mark of a veteran is not whether mistakes happen, but how gracefully recovery occurs. Leadership is no different. You will misjudge, misread, or intervene too late. Repair matters more than failure.

Repair says: I see it. I own it. I'm coming back with clarity, not excuses.

Repair is how leaders earn people back.

With time, the fear doesn't disappear, but it softens. I have always believed that discomfort means I still care. I once told my wife, "When the hard conversations get easy, I'm done. It means I no longer care."

Facing the music is not about bracing yourself.
It is about opening yourself.

It is believed that people deserve your clarity more than your smoothness. It is understood that truth delivered with dignity carries its own quiet mercy.

“I learned everything from listening to other people.”

Eric Clapton

CHAPTER 27:

Who Is Your Conductor?

In an orchestra, the conductor never plays a single note. No one instrument belongs to them, yet the entire performance responds to their guidance. Their hands do not create sound, but they shape it, the phrasing, the timing, and the emotional color. A conductor listens more than they lead. They adjust without speaking. Their presence is not loud, yet it holds the room.

Musicians know the difference a good conductor makes. Under one, a song feels rigid and technical. Under another, it comes alive, warmer, more human, more expressive. The musicians are the same. The notes are the same. What changes is the influence.

Leadership is no different.

Every leader, whether they recognize it or not, is being conducted by someone.

Some conductors are visible: mentors, supervisors, colleagues whose wisdom steadies your own. Others are internal: voices from your past, values you inherited, lessons you learned the hard way. Some uplift. Some restrict. Some you choose intentionally. Others you carry without realizing it.

Early in my career, I believed independence was the hallmark of leadership. I thought strong leaders carved their own paths, trusted their instincts, and relied solely on their own judgment. Over time, experience corrected me. Influence is unavoidable. We are all shaped by someone's baton.

The question is not whether you have a conductor. The question is whether you have chosen the right one or ones.

Leadership writers often remind us that leadership is influence, and that growth requires proximity to people who embody the kind of leadership we aspire to. However it is phrased, the principle holds: with whom you walk shapes who you become.

Dr. Heuser, a professor I had at Plymouth State University, gave language to this when he used a word I have never forgotten, furtherer, a person who consistently encourages your growth, personally or professionally. Everyone needs a furtherer. Everyone needs someone who helps them grow toward who they could become.

I remember the first person who truly conducted my leadership. I was teaching kindergarten. He wasn't my supervisor, but when he entered a room, the energy shifted, not through authority, but through presence. He listened slowly. He spoke sparingly. He corrected gently. He often began with, "Help me understand...."

Without intending to, I began mirroring him, his steadiness, his curiosity, his refusal to escalate tension. His influence didn't turn me into a copy of him. It revealed a version of leadership I didn't know I could inhabit. To his credit, I still quote him to teachers today, nearly three decades later.

Later, I encountered a very different kind of conductor.

His leadership was clipped, reactive, and perpetually braced for crisis. He was intelligent, well-read, and fluent in the language of leadership, yet, in practice, he distorted the very principles he admired. Instead of inspiring confidence, he created tension. Colleagues quietly placed bets on whether he would lose it in meetings. Whatever his message was, it rarely reached its destination.

Around him, my own tone shifted. I became sharper, more impatient, more defensive. My instinct was not to listen, but to brace. It took years and humility to recognize that I had allowed someone else's anxiety to set my rhythm.

Influence works both ways.

Good conductors elevate you. Poor conductors distort you.

Leadership asks you to notice the difference honestly, without flattery or blame. Name it. Own it. Then deal with it.

- Who shapes your timing?
- Who regulates your emotional tempo?
- Whose approval or disapproval lingers in your decisions?
- Whose style echoes in your tone?

These questions matter because leadership is never solo work. Even when you stand alone in front of a room, you carry the teachings, habits, scars, and wisdom of those who influenced you. You play with their phrasing in your fingers.

The most significant shift in my leadership came when I became intentional about the voices I allowed to conduct me. I sought people who brought steadiness rather than speed, clarity rather than noise, courage rather than caution. Mentors who knew when to push and when to protect.

At one point, I completed an exercise that changed me: I listed every leader I had worked under, their names, their strengths, and how they shaped my leadership. Patterns emerged. So did hard truths. Their influence did not replace my voice; it refined it.

Students have conductors, too, teachers who shape confidence, adults who shape a sense of safety. When mentorship becomes intentional rather than accidental, entire communities grow healthier. People learn to recognize which voices guide them, and to choose those that align with their best selves.

Leadership is influence. Wise leadership is choosing your influences.

Eventually, quietly, without announcement, you will become a conductor for others. Not by waving a baton or giving orders, but by embodying a tone worth following. Your calm becomes their grounding. Your integrity becomes their cue.

You begin to understand that leadership is less about directing the music and more about shaping the conditions under which others can play their best.

Over time, the most important question shifts. It is no longer "Who is my conductor?"

It becomes: Whose sound am I shaping, without even realizing it?

Which brings me back to Dr. Heuser's word: furtherer. It has guided my career as an ethical stance. I want to help people grow. I want to help them find the version of themselves that plays most honestly.

I hope that, along the way, I have been a furtherer for a few remarkable people, too.

"If you're going to be a rock star, go be one. People don't want to see the guy next door on stage; they want to see somebody from another planet."

Lemmy Kilmister (Motörhead)

CHAPTER 28:
Stage Fright Is a Leadership Skill

There is a moment, just before stepping onto any stage, when even seasoned performers feel a flicker of fear. A tightening in the stomach. A small catch in the breath. A whisper of doubt: What if this time I'm not enough? Musicians call it stage fright, but that label is too narrow. It isn't just fear. It is awareness, the sudden recognition that what you are about to do matters.

I first felt it as a leader, not during a keynote or a high-stakes meeting, but in a quiet conversation with a student who needed me to be steady when I wasn't sure I could be. I felt that familiar tightening, not panic, but presence. The sense that the moment carried weight. That I needed to rise into it.

That day, I learned something essential: stage fright isn't a barrier to be removed. It is a messenger. It says, Pay attention. Bring your whole self. This matters.

Musicians understand this instinctively. Nerves sharpen the senses. They heighten awareness. They pull you fully into the present. Neuroscience confirms what performers have long known: anxiety and focus share pathways. The same surge that makes us nervous also primes us for attention. Without it, we drift. We perform on autopilot. We lose the edge that makes the moment honest.

Even legends feel it. Before his first major post-Beatles performance, the 1969 Toronto Rock and Roll Revival with the Plastic Ono Band, John Lennon reportedly vomited backstage from anxiety. Despite years of touring and global acclaim, stepping onto a stage without the band's familiar safety unsettled him deeply. Yet he walked on anyway. Leaders do the same, not because they feel fearless, but because they feel responsible.

Leadership works this way.
That racing pulse before a difficult conversation means the relationship matters.
That flutter before addressing a fractured team means trust is at stake.
That doubt before giving hard feedback means your words carry weight.

The goal is not to numb these signals. It is to understand them.

Stage fright reveals values. It marks the moments where presence can steady or shape another person. People often misread nerves as weakness, but in leadership, as in performance, nerves are evidence of responsibility. They are the trembling edge of courage.

I have known leaders who tried to suppress the feeling, treating it as something to conquer or hide. But the leaders who inspired me most carried their nerves with humility. They didn't apologize for them. They didn't dramatize them. They allowed the feeling to sharpen their focus. Their vulnerability made them more human. Their humanity made them more trustworthy.

I once watched a new teacher speak at a school assembly. Her hands shook and her voice wavered at the edges, but her message was honest and her intention was clear. The applause that followed wasn't for polish. It was for bravery. Later, she apologized for being nervous. What she didn't realize was that her nerves made her message land more deeply. Her vulnerability created a connection.

That is the quiet truth about stage fright: it humanizes you. It closes the distance. It proves investment.

When leaders pretend to feel nothing, they create distance. Stoicism without sincerity alienates. Emotional flooding overwhelms. Authenticity steadies. The work is not performance, it is presence.

Stage fright is not the enemy of leadership. It is the companion of authenticity.

Once you understand that, you stop bracing against the nerves. You stop treating them as a flaw. You begin to recognize them as a signal that the moment deserves your full attention.

Leadership, at its core, is stepping onto countless small stages, classrooms, hallways, offices, difficult conversations, and offering something true, even when your hands shake a little.

The leaders people trust most are not the ones who feel nothing.

They are the ones who feel enough to show up fully anyway.

"I've got tinnitus… ringing in the ears… and I wish I'd taken better care."

Eric Clapton

Some of the greatest musicians in history lost their hearing not because they lacked talent, but because they ignored the limits of their own instrument. Leadership works the same way. If you don't manage the volume, you eventually lose the ability to hear.

CHAPTER 29:
Volume Does Not Equal Leadership

There is a temptation, especially early in leadership, to believe that influence comes from volume. In music, the loudest instrument often seems to command the room: the driving drum line, the soaring guitar solo, the full-voiced singer. Anyone who has stood too close to a speaker at a concert knows the truth. Volume can overwhelm without ever connecting. It can be loud without being meaningful.

Quiet musicians understand something different. Influence has very little to do with decibels. A soft, finger-picked guitar can hush a crowded room. A breathy vocal can pull an audience closer. A single sustained note can still fill an entire theater. Power can be gentle, and gentle power often lingers longer.

When a beloved teacher at our school passed away, our staff read Susan Cain's Quiet: The Power of Introverts in a World That Can't Stop Talking to better understand him. He was deeply respected but rarely loud. A teacher-leader suggested the book, and the school purchased copies. We weren't reading to study introversion; we were trying to understand someone we admired in retrospect.

The message landed hard. The loudest voice is not necessarily the wisest. There is no correlation between being the best talker and having the best ideas. Quiet people often carry depth that gets missed in noisy rooms, not because they lack insight, but because their inner world is reflective, observant, and generative.

The invitation isn't to push quiet leaders to perform like loud ones. It's to honor their wiring as a strength. The work of naturally noisy leaders isn't to fix quiet people; it's to make space for them, to slow the tempo, listen differently, and recognize that insight often speaks softly before it resonates.

Quiet leadership is often misunderstood. Gentleness is mistaken for weakness, humility for hesitation, calm for lack of conviction. I've learned, however, that quiet leaders often carry the deepest strength, a strength rooted not in domination, but in presence.

I have seen loud leadership. It can energize briefly, but it rarely sustains. Volume can wake people up, but it rarely invites them in. Loud leaders often mistake noise for momentum. They push when listening is needed. They speak when silence would offer more truth. They try to convince rather than connect.

By contrast, I have watched quiet leaders transform entire teams. They do it through consistency, meeting people where they are, offering a steady tone, choosing words that strengthen rather than bruise. Their calm becomes emotional architecture. People feel safer. They bring fuller versions of themselves because the room feels held rather than driven.

There was a teacher, soft-spoken, her voice barely reaching the back of the auditorium, who held more authority with students than anyone else in the building. She didn't command the room; she invited it. Students didn't need volume to feel guided. They needed sincerity. When they entered her classroom, even the loudest softened. Years later, former students spoke less about what she taught and more about how she made them feel: steady, noticed, capable.

Volume didn't make her a leader. Presence did.

In leadership, loudness is often a mask, hiding uncertainty or fear. Clarity, compassion, and conviction require no amplification. Lowering your volume can be an act of confidence. It signals trust in yourself, in others, in the room.

There are moments when firmness is necessary, when safety demands clarity or boundaries need sharp edges. Even then, though, volume isn't the point. Precision is. Quiet leaders don't disappear; they refine. That refinement, steady, intentional, humane, creates a kind of leadership people return to because it feels like truth rather than performance.

When I think about the leaders who shaped me most, they weren't the loud ones. They were the ones whose tone matched their values. The ones who didn't need to shout to be heard. The ones who understood that leadership isn't the amplification of self, but the creation of space where others can rise.

In music, the most powerful moment is often the softest.

Leadership is no different

"If you don't keep your guitar in tune, nothing else matters."

Eddie Van Halen

CHAPTER 30:
Tuning Between Songs

If you watch a live performance closely, you'll notice what happens between songs. The crowd may be cheering, the lights shifting, the atmosphere swelling, but the musicians pause to tune. It is quick, almost invisible: a peg turned, a string stretched, a breath taken. Sometimes a new guitar appears, handed off by a technician the audience barely sees. The room may not notice, but the band does. They know that a single song played out of tune can fracture the arc of the night.

Those quiet moments between songs matter. They are the reset.

Leadership has its own version of tuning, small, subtle adjustments made in public that keep you aligned with the leader you intend to be. These corrections aren't dramatic. They don't require announcements or explanations. They happen in the in-between spaces, often in full view of others, yet private in a way only you can feel.

I learned the importance of this after one of the most difficult conversations of my career. A parent phoned, shaken and frightened, explaining that their child had come home with soreness in their private parts. They believed it had occurred on the school bus. As they spoke, fear quickly turned to accusation. When the call ended, I was left holding weight, trying to process what might have happened, what the mandated reporting laws were in Kuwait, what needed to occur immediately, and what the next day would bring.

I scribbled notes for follow-up and rushed straight into a faculty meeting I was scheduled to lead. The topic was curriculum alignment, teaching from standards using Jay McTighe's Understanding by Design framework.

Partway through the meeting, a teacher at the back raised her hand. "How are we supposed to teach this way when the kids neither write nor speak in English? This is supposed to be an American school."

No one in that room knew what had just been placed on my shoulder's minutes earlier, and, instead of tuning myself before stepping in, I reacted.

"Come on. Don't be stupid," I snapped, a sentence I regretted before it finished leaving my mouth.

I knew immediately I was off-key. I asked another teacher to guide the discussion while I steadied myself. Later, I apologized, privately and publicly, acknowledging that I had not been in the right mindset to lead that meeting. What I needed before entering that room was exactly what any musician needs between songs: a retune. A new guitar. A breath. A recalibration.

(As a side note, that teacher and I eventually became good friends, proof that repair, when done well, can deepen trust.)

That day taught me something lasting: leadership is filled with moments that function like tuning. Small corrections where you pull yourself back into alignment, recognizing that you are not quite where you want to be and choosing, without drama or self-punishment, to make it right.

This is the quiet work of leadership. You do it when you walk into a meeting carrying frustration and decide not to pass it on to others. You do it when your voice rises too quickly, and you soften it mid-sentence. You do it when you begin a conversation distracted, notice it, and refocus on the person in front of you. You do it when you feel yourself closing and choose to stay open instead.

These are not grand gestures. They are the equivalent of nudging a tuning peg until the pitch settles.

What I love about this metaphor is that musicians never apologize for tuning; they simply do it. They understand that tuning is an act of professionalism, of respect for the craft, for their bandmates, and for the audience listening.

Leaders benefit from that same humility. Rarely do we arrive perfectly in tune. We tune as we go. We adjust. We recover. Being human means drifting, not failing.

Because leadership is visible, those micro-adjustments matter. People notice how you regulate yourself. They notice when you correct your tone. They notice when you choose steadiness over impulse. This is modeling at its best, not perfection, but responsibility.

I have learned more about leadership by watching people recover than by watching them perform. The strongest leaders are not the ones who never drift off-key. They are the ones who tune quickly, gently, without shame.

Over time, tuning between songs becomes instinctive. You feel when something is slightly off, your patience, your presence, your focus, and you realign before the next moment begins. Not because you are performing, but because you understand that what you bring into the room becomes part of the room.

Leadership is not shaped only by the big moments.
It is shaped by how willing you are to tune between them.

Even on stage, great band leaders sense when the band needs a beat. They tell a story. Hold silence. Speak to the crowd just long enough for their bandmates to adjust. They don't fill the pause with ego; they fill it with awareness.

Great leaders do the same. They sense when their people need space to retune, and they give it.

INTERLUDE:
The Talent Show Trumpet Story

There was a student once, a small, wiry fifth grader named Alex (I will call him that), who signed up for the talent show carrying a trumpet nearly as big as he was. He wasn't particularly skilled yet. His tone wavered, his fingers fumbled, and he had a habit of closing his eyes every time he played, as if the notes were safer when he couldn't see where they landed.

On the day of the show, he waited backstage, clutching the trumpet with both hands, bouncing lightly on his toes. When his name was called, he froze. Not dramatically. No tears. Just a quiet stillness that said, I'm not sure I can do this anymore.

A teacher leaned down and whispered, "You don't have to be perfect. You just have to be brave."

He nodded, stepped onto the stage, and lifted the trumpet with trembling hands. The first note cracked loudly. A few kids giggled. He winced, eyes filling, holding the trumpet high as if it might hide his face. It was panic, plain and simple.

As the principal, and as someone who had played trumpet at his age, I knew exactly what he was feeling.

I stepped onto the stage and stood beside him.
"Alex," I said gently, "maybe something's wrong with the trumpet. Mind if I try it?"

He hesitated, then handed it to me.

I puffed out my cheeks and tried to make that trumpet sing. I failed spectacularly. My face reddened. The sound was awful.

"You're doing it all wrong," Alex announced, suddenly confident. "Give it back."

He took the trumpet and showed me how it was supposed to be done.

He made it through the entire piece, wobbling in and out of tune, but never stepping off the stage. When he finished, the auditorium held a beat of silence and then erupted into applause far bigger than the performance itself.

He walked offstage red-faced and smiling, the trumpet suddenly lighter in his hands.

What moved me wasn't the music. It was the courage.

Leadership has moments like this, too.
Moments when the spotlight finds you before you feel ready.
Moments when your voice cracks or your confidence wavers.

Moments when your uncertainty is more visible than you'd like.

And still, you stay.

Not because you are flawless, but because you understand that showing up imperfectly matters more than delivering a perfect performance. People don't need your polish. They need your presence.

That student taught me something I never forgot. Courage doesn't sound clean. It sounds human.

Sometimes the most important leadership moments begin with one cracked note you choose to play anyway.

Part V: LEGACY, MENTORSHIP, AND VOICE

Visibility, Courage, and Consequence

CHAPTER 31:

You Are More Than Your Greatest Hits

Well-known musicians often reach a moment when people begin to associate them with a single song. It might be the breakout track, the anthem that filled stadiums, or the ballad that made strangers cry. It becomes the request shouted from balconies, the encore audiences wait for, the song people believe somehow explains the artist's identity.

There is pride in that, real pride. There is also a quiet pressure that settles in: What if this is all they ever see in me? What if my best work is already behind me?

Leaders feel a version of this as well.

There are moments in your career when you do something meaningful, something that steadies a teacher, protects a child, strengthens a community, and people begin to define you by that moment. They say things like, "Remember when you handled that crisis so well?" or "You're the one who built that program," or "You always know how to calm a room."

It is affirming.
It is earned.
It can also be limiting.

As humans, we are always evolving, and we deserve to be known as more than our highlights. We can say, "Who I was is not necessarily who I am, and who I am today does not limit who I will become."

Early in my career, a single success followed me wherever I went. I became known as the Environmental Guy, the leader who organized an annual walk-a-thon celebrating "the earth we walk on, the oceans we see, the air we breathe, the water we drink, and respect for human beings," all in one remarkable week.

It was a phenomenal event, better than I had imagined. People kept referring to it. Meetings, introductions, even casual hallway conversations circled around that moment as if it were definitive proof of who I was as an educator and leader.

But it wasn't the whole story of my leadership.

Over time, I felt a strange tension: gratitude for the recognition, and a quiet ache that no one could see the ways I was still learning, stretching, and growing beyond that moment. Of course, I cared deeply about the environment, but I also wanted to be seen as an educational leader.

That was when I realized something important: being defined by your best work can become a trap of its own. Your greatest hits aren't false; they are simply not your entire oeuvre.

Leadership, like music, is a lifelong creative act. Every season adds a new tone, new texture, new truth. Some years bring bold, resonant chords. Others offer quieter, more introspective passages. Some expand your range. Others deepen it.

You are not meant to repeat your greatest hits forever.
You are meant to grow past them.

The students who need you now are not living in the moment that earned you praise five years ago. The colleagues who rely on you are shaped not by your past accomplishments, but by the presence you bring today. Communities evolve, and leaders must evolve with them.

When you cling too tightly to old success, you stop allowing yourself to become the leader you are still becoming.

I came to realize something essential: I do not want to play the same song in every room I enter. I want to bring the version of myself that belongs in that room.

That realization freed me from chasing the echo of what I had already done and invited me to attend to the moment right in front of me.

The truth is this: your legacy will never be a single moment, not even a brilliant one.

It is built on a long line of moments people rarely notice, staying a little longer after school to listen, choosing integrity when no one is watching, returning to steadiness after a mistake, offering quiet courage when it matters most. These moments rarely make the highlight reel, but they shape a life. They become the thread that weaves character.

Your greatest hits matter. They show what you are capable of. They light the path behind you.

But they are not the edge of your identity.
They are simply early songs in an album still being written.

You are allowed to evolve.
You are allowed to grow.
You are allowed to outgrow even the best version of your past self.

Leadership, true leadership, is not about who you have been. It is about who you are becoming and the music you have not yet played.

There is one final truth worth holding alongside this one: we should not be judged, nor should we judge others, by our worst days either. Those moments do not define us any more than our greatest hits do. What matters most is the recovery.

Even if all someone ever saw was your lowest note, the deeper question remains: Who did you become because of it?

That is the fuller measure of growth and the truer story of leadership.

CHAPTER 32:
Set Up Your Own Gear

Among serious musicians, there is an unspoken professional norm: you set up your own gear.

You arrive early. You tune deliberately. You check cables and connections. You test the monitors and adjust the strap. You make sure the instrument you carry onto the stage can hold tension. No audience sees this work. It is quiet, almost mundane. But every audience experiences the consequences of whether it was done well.

Leadership operates by the same discipline.

Before influence is exercised, before a decision is announced, before a difficult conversation begins, a leader must do work that is largely invisible. Setting up your own gear is the discipline of readiness before action. It is not charisma. It is not inspiration. It is preparation. It is the deliberate alignment of thinking, emotion, and posture so that when the moment arrives, your presence is steady.

Early in my leadership journey, I mistook readiness for confidence. If I felt intellectually clear, I assumed I was prepared. I learned, often uncomfortably, that clarity of thought does not guarantee stability of presence. You can be correct in principle and still unready in posture. You can have the right decision and deliver it poorly. You can carry good intentions into a room and allow fatigue or defensiveness to shape the tone.

Readiness has layers. It requires technical preparation: facts gathered, documentation reviewed, policy understood, expectations clarified. It requires emotional preparation: awareness of your own stress level, the triggers likely to surface, the habits you default to under pressure. And it requires relational preparation: anticipating how your words may land, who will experience loss or disappointment, and what unspoken concerns may surface once the conversation begins.

When one of these layers is neglected, strain shows.

I remember entering an early parent meeting with goodwill but without documentation. My reasoning was sound. My intentions were sincere. But when emotion escalated, I found myself defending memory rather than grounding the conversation in evidence. The meeting did not collapse, but it tightened unnecessarily. Trust thinned at the edges. The issue was not the decision. The issue was the gear.

Setting up your own gear also requires pre-commitment. Before entering complexity, leaders must quietly decide who they intend to be when the pressure rises. What value will anchor you if the conversation becomes uncomfortable? What tone will you protect if someone challenges your judgment? What boundary will you hold if pushed? Without pre-commitment, leaders default to instinct. Under pressure, instinct is rarely aspirational. It is reactive. Gear protects integrity under tension because it has been tuned in advance.

Musicians understand that once the set begins, it is too late to restring the instrument. Leaders must understand the same principle. Once a meeting is live, once a conversation is charged, once the decision is public, your preparation either holds or it does not. You cannot pause the exchange to recalibrate your emotional state. You cannot retroactively gather the facts you should have reviewed. You cannot reclaim a tone that slipped because you entered the room uncentered.

There is also a myth that readiness can be outsourced. It cannot. You can delegate tasks. You can share leadership. You can distribute execution. But you cannot delegate the responsibility of showing up grounded, clear, and composed. Teams amplify tone; they do not stabilize it. If a leader arrives rushed, ambiguous, or emotionally frayed, that energy multiplies. If a leader arrives measured and prepared, that steadiness spreads just as quickly.

Setting up your own gear is, therefore, a professional act of respect. It respects the work enough to approach it deliberately. It respects the people involved enough to offer them clarity instead of improvisation. It respects the role enough to recognize that authority carries with it an obligation.

This string in the Power Chords model lives before visible leadership. It exists in the parking lot before you walk into the building. It exists in the quiet review of notes before a conversation. It exists in the internal question asked before responding: Am I ready to carry this well?

Gear is readiness before action.

It ensures that when the first chord is struck, when the meeting begins, when the announcement is made, when the tension surfaces, the instrument you bring does not betray the values you claim. Preparation is rarely celebrated. It does not generate applause. But its absence is unmistakable.

Preparation is invisible.
Its absence never is.

"I felt like a beginner again."

Neil Peart

After working with jazz teacher Freddie Gruber in the 1990s, Peart rebuilt his technique and feel.

CHAPTER 33:
The Student Who Changed My Ear

As musicians grow in their craft, the way in which they listen to music changes.

Sometimes it happens when you discover a new genre. Sometimes a teacher points out a detail you had been missing. Sometimes it comes quietly, through an experience that expands your capacity to hear what was always there. Your ear shifts. Your understanding widens. You begin to pick up harmonics, textures, and tensions that once passed unnoticed.

A student once did that for me, not by teaching me anything about music, but by reshaping the way I listened to people.

He was not a standout personality. He was not loud, troubled, precocious, or especially visible. He was one of those students who moved through school invisibly competent, polite, steady, easy to categorize as "doing fine." For months, I interacted with him the way adults often do with quiet achievers: warmly, but without much curiosity. Because he never required attention, I assumed he didn't need much from me.

One afternoon, I noticed him sitting alone in the courtyard. That was not unusual, but something about his posture made me pause, the way you stop when you hear a note that is technically correct but emotionally off. I sat beside him without pushing or prying, just sharing the space.

After a moment, he said quietly,

"I'm not really sure how to say this."

His voice was steady, but unguarded. He told me he often felt invisible, not mistreated, just unseen. Adults praised his independence without realizing that much of it came from believing there wasn't room for him to need anything.

That brief conversation tuned something in me.

He was not asking for intervention. He was not asking to be fixed. What he wanted was resonance, someone to notice the subtleties of his experience, not just the surface performance. Listening to him felt like hearing a harmony line I had missed for years. He taught me that many students move between success and struggle unheard, simply because they do not make noise about their needs.

In music, power is not always complexity. Power chords work because they are simple, grounded, and unmistakable. They cut through not by being intricate, but by being true. What that student offered me was a "power chord," a clean, honest signal that revealed how much I had been listening for volume instead of resonance.

A few weeks later, I asked the teachers for help with an exercise. I created a list of every student in the school and asked staff to place a check beside each student they truly knew, not by reputation or performance, but in depth: their motivations, fears, hopes, and strengths.

Some names had multiple checks.
Some had one.
A few had none.

The list was unsettling. The students with the fewest checks were often the quietest, most compliant, most "successful." They were easy to overlook precisely because they caused no disruption. The exercise became another power chord, simple, unmistakable, and impossible to ignore.

From that day on, I began listening differently. Not just to what students said, but to pauses. To shifts in tone. To posture. To those who grew quieter around certain adults. To those who never raised their hand but always stayed after class. My leadership ear sharpened, not dramatically, but in the way musicians develop in their craft over time, learning to hear the chord beneath the melody.

Years later, I ran into that student again. He was older, more confident, more present in his own life. He thanked me for that courtyard moment. The truth is, I owe him thanks.

Bands know that music is rarely carried by what is loudest. The parts that change a song often sit beneath the surface, unnoticed until something inside you shifts and you finally hear them. Leadership is the same. We respond to volume, crisis, brilliance, conflict, drama, but the moments that shape us most arrive quietly.

That student did not teach me by instructing me. He taught me by trusting me.

Since then, I carry his lesson into every meeting, every hallway greeting, every conversation: listen beyond loudness, especially when the room is full of data, dashboards, urgency, or noise. Hear the rests as clearly as the notes. Pay attention to the simple, true signals people rarely name out loud.

Power chords are not flashy. They are not complicated. But once you hear them, the whole song changes.

And once your ear changes, it never goes back.

CHAPTER 34:
Write Songs Only You Can Write

Many musicians begin to play by covering songs they love. It is how you learn, copying chords, mimicking tone, imitating phrasing, shaping your sound inside someone else's framework. There is nothing wrong with that. In fact, it is essential. Capability is built on the scaffolding of another artist's wisdom. There comes a moment, though, sometimes early, sometimes painfully late, when you realize you cannot stay inside someone else's sound forever.

At some point, you must write something that belongs only to you. Something shaped by your history, your wiring, your contradictions, your truth. Something that carries your imperfections and fingerprints.

Leadership mirrors this journey.

We all begin by imitating those who shaped us. I certainly did. In my early years, I borrowed tone, language, and approach, sometimes without even realizing it. One season, I mirrored the confident decisiveness of a supervisor I admired. Another, I tried on the quiet wisdom of a colleague whose calm could steady any room. At other times, I mimicked leaders who spoke boldly, assuming volume meant courage.

Eventually, imitation becomes uncomfortable. It is like wearing clothes tailored for someone else, close, but never quite right. You find yourself striving instead of leading, performing instead of connecting.

Slowly, a truth emerges that many leaders discover the hard way:

You cannot lead well using someone else's voice.
Your leadership must sound like you.

This realization arrived for me during a year when I felt particularly stretched. I was in a new role, surrounded by strong personalities, each rooted in their own style. I tried to match them, more forceful, more polished, more certain. It was not dishonest, but it was performative. I felt like I was playing songs written for someone else.

After a difficult meeting where I forced a tone that was not mine, a colleague pulled me aside and said gently, "You don't have to sound like them."

The comment was simple, kind, almost throwaway, but it struck me like a tuning fork. I suddenly recognized how much energy I was spending trying to sound like other people's definition of leadership.

I stepped back. I listened for my own voice, the way I made sense of things, the way I connected, the way I navigated complexity. I noticed that my most meaningful leadership moments did not come when I sounded impressive. They came when I sounded honest.

This matters even more now.

We are entering a leadership era shaped by tools that can imitate voice, style, tone, and reasoning at remarkable speed. Artificial intelligence can draft messages, summarize conflict, generate plans, and offer polished language on demand. Used well, it can support leaders. Used poorly, it can hollow them out.

There is a growing temptation to let tools do the sounding for us, but leadership is not automation.

AI can help leaders think, but it cannot decide what matters. It can assist, but its input cannot carry moral weight. It can make suggestions, but it cannot replace judgment. When leaders outsource their voices too quickly, they risk losing the very thing that makes people trust them: presence, discernment, and accountability.

The most credible guidance emerging around AI in education returns to this same principle: technology should act as a co-pilot, not an autopilot. Tools may support human thinking, but responsibility and authorship must remain human. Leadership, especially in schools, is still relational, ethical, and deeply contextual.

Students sense this immediately. They recognize borrowed tone faster than adults do. They know when you are performing, and they respond most deeply when you show up as yourself, steady, imperfect, grounded.

Writing songs that only you can write does not mean rejecting influence or tools. It means weaving the wisdom of others, and the assistance of technology, through lived experience until something original emerges. It means honoring mentors and methods without surrendering authorship.

Your leadership voice is made from every place you have lived, every mistake you have made, every mentor who nudged you forward, and every child who trusted you. It is built from conviction and uncertainty, confidence and curiosity. It is not perfect, but it is yours.

The world does not need another imitation.
It does not need another polished script.

It needs leaders who can think with tools without being swallowed by them. Leaders who can use assistance without surrendering agency. Leaders who remain unmistakably human in an age of increasingly convincing replicas.

So, write the songs only you can write, slowly, imperfectly, with the full weight of your experience behind them. Write them with humility. Write them with conviction. Write them knowing your voice matters not because it is flawless, but because it is authentic.

When you do, something remarkable happens: people hear a tone they did not know they were waiting for, the unmistakable sound of a leader who has finally found their own voice.

CHAPTER 35:
Know Thy Impact

Every musician knows that the final note of a song is not its true ending. Sound lingers. It softens into the air and becomes vibration. What remains is not volume, but impact.

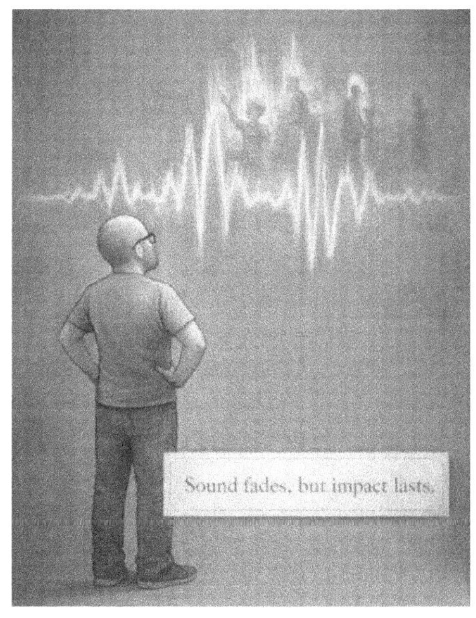

Leadership leaves an impact long before it leaves memory.

Educational researcher John Hattie urges leaders to "know thy impact" (Hattie, 2012). This is not merely a measurement challenge. It is an ethical one. Leaders must understand the effect of their decisions, not only on outcomes, but on people.

Impact is not abstract. It is embodied.

It lives in whether teachers feel safe to speak.
In whether students risk trying again.
In whether meetings invite honesty or silence.
In whether disagreement feels dangerous or developmental.

Long after policies are revised and programs are replaced, tone remains.

I understood this most clearly when I returned to a school years after leaving it. The building had changed. The staff had shifted. The systems were updated. Yet something felt familiar: the steadiness of conversations, the transparency in meetings, the way conflict was handled without theatrics. Not because it was "mine," but because tone had outlasted tenure.

That is impact.

You do not control it completely.
You influence it continuously.

Most leaders focus on visible initiatives. But culture forms around repeated micro-choices: a calm response under stress, an apology without qualification, a boundary held without humiliation, a decision explained rather than imposed.

These accumulate. Leadership teaches whether you intend it or not.

Resonance, in this sense, is not legacy. It is a lived alignment. It is the coherence between what you say matters and what your behavior consistently signals.

Scholars of organizational change remind us that culture shifts through modeling, not mandate. People watch how leaders behave when the stakes are real. They look for congruence under pressure. Over time, that congruence becomes trust.

The question is not whether you have impact.

The question is whether you are paying attention to it.

Resonance begins here, not at the end of your career, but in the daily discipline of knowing the sound you are contributing to the room.

CHAPTER 36:
Teach the Band to Play Without You

Every musician eventually learns an uncomfortable truth: the music goes on even when they are not on stage. Bands survive lineup changes. Songs still get played. Audiences keep listening. The world rarely stops when one person steps away; sometimes, it barely pauses.

The first time you encounter this truth, it can bruise the ego. When you sit out a rehearsal, and the band plays just fine, it is tempting to feel replaced rather than proud. But the bands that last, the ones that mature, are not built around a single indispensable player. They are built so the sound can travel without them.

Leadership is no different.

Early in your career, being needed feels affirming. People seek you out. They wait for your opinion. They defer to your judgment. It feels like influence; it masquerades as importance. If you are not careful, it becomes identity. You begin to believe the day depends on you.

Over time, a humbling truth surfaces:

If everything falls apart without you, you haven't built leadership; you've built dependency.

I spent years quietly being the fixer. If a crisis surfaced, it landed on my desk. If a decision felt difficult, people waited for me to make it. If someone hesitated, I stepped in. None of this was driven by ego; it was habit. The school had learned that I would always rise, and I had learned to let it expect me to do so.

One afternoon, after yet another solvable issue appeared in my inbox, something shifted. Not irritation, awareness.

This shouldn't depend on me.

In that moment, I realized I had unintentionally trained people to rely on me more than they relied on themselves. Few leadership lessons are more sobering than discovering you have become the bottleneck to the growth you hoped to create.

Bands collapse under leaders convinced they are irreplaceable. The healthiest ensembles, whether a jazz trio improvising without a bass line or an orchestra continuing when the conductor steps aside, play well because leadership is distributed rather than hoarded. They rehearse transitions.

They teach one another the parts. They build resilience into the arrangement.

So, I began to step back, not away, but back far enough for others to step forward.

When someone asked what to do, I asked what they thought might work.
When staff sought reassurance before acting, I offered principles rather than prescriptions.
When colleagues deferred too quickly, I let the silence hold long enough for someone else to find their voice.

At first, people hesitated. Muscles that had never been exercised trembled. Gradually, something remarkable happened: they trusted themselves. When people trust themselves, the environment shifts, initiative rises, collaboration strengthens, and confidence flows outward instead of upward.

The band begins to sound like a band, not a soloist with accompaniment.

This shift requires humility. It means relinquishing the intoxicating feeling of being indispensable. It requires patience, because people falter as they grow. It asks you to resist rescuing every moment. It demands you face a truth which leaders rarely say aloud:

The music will continue without you, and that is the point.

Leadership worth honoring does not end with you. It expands beyond you. Students sense this immediately. They know when a school's strength lives inside a single person versus when it runs through the culture. They thrive where capability is shared rather than guarded.

There is a quiet joy in hearing someone else carry a moment you once held, not because you became unnecessary, but because you became generative. You multiplied yourself through others.

The first time I watched someone navigate a crisis without me, I felt something I didn't expect: relief, tinged with a sense of irrelevance. Beneath that discomfort was the sound of something healthy, leadership maturing beyond the limits of a single voice.

One day, you will walk out of your office, whether for an afternoon, a sabbatical, or the last time, and the real measure of your leadership will be revealed in what happens next. Does the rhythm collapse? Or does it continue, evolving through voices you helped strengthen?

If the band can play without you, you did it right.

Not because you made yourself indispensable, but because you made others capable.

That is the quiet genius of leadership: you spend years building a sound you will not always be there to conduct. If you have led well, intentionally, humbly, generously, the music will not end when you leave.

It will deepen.
It will widen.
It will travel farther than you ever could.

That, in the end, is the most enduring solo you will never play.

INTERLUDE:
The Notes No One Saw Me Write

Once, as a head of school, I arrived long before sunrise, 4:30 a.m., with a stack of Post-it notes and a black marker. It had been a heavy season. The weeks prior had carried more than the usual academic pressure. A student's illness. A disciplinary situation that strained friendships. College decisions looming. Faculty fatigue that students could feel even if they could not name it. Nothing catastrophic. Just accumulation. The kind of emotional weather that lowers a building by a few invisible degrees.

In the stillness of empty corridors, I wrote simple messages on 325 lockers:

You are loved.
Hang in there.
You've got this.

A small smiley face. Nothing elaborate. Nothing traceable back to me.

I didn't sign the notes. There was no announcement, no recognition. The point was never visibility. The point was presence, how a small, unexpected word can recalibrate the emotional climate of a building that has grown tight.

In hindsight, it felt like laying down a supporting track in a song: a bass line no one applauds but everyone feels. Some of the most meaningful contributions in a band are the ones that hold the music together quietly. A harmony that warms the room. A drummer who steadies the pulse. A technician who tunes instruments backstage so someone else can shine under the lights.

Those Post-its were not decorations. They were calibrated.

The next morning, I watched from a distance as students opened lockers and paused. Some smiled. Some took pictures. Some folded the notes and tucked them into backpacks. One student stood still for a long moment before slipping the note into a binder. The building sounded different that day, not louder, but lighter, as if someone had adjusted the tone without anyone knowing who did it.

That moment clarified something for me: the heart of leadership is not only direction or visibility. It is an atmosphere.

Students do not only carry schedules and assignments. They carry uncertainty, comparison, private fear, and the constant question of whether they belong. In difficult seasons, belonging becomes fragile. And when belonging thins, performance follows.

No algorithm can sense the emotional weather of a school and choose to soften it.
No machine can leave a quiet word that steadies a child.

Technology can optimize function. Only people can tune in to a sense of belonging.

The leadership ahead of us will demand more than skill. It will require attentiveness, discretion, and the discipline to notice climate before crisis. Future-ready ensembles, schools, teams, communities, will not be defined by the virtuoso at center stage, but by their ability to stay in time with one another when the spotlight shifts.

I didn't sign those notes, and that was intentional. Leadership in the coming era will be less about being seen and more about being responsible, less about performance and more about cultivating conditions where others learn to lead.

If you can brighten one person's day, do it. If you can quietly stabilize many, even better. And if you can grow a culture where people begin to encourage one another through gestures you may never witness, then you have not just led the band: you have prepared it for the future.

PART VI: REFLECTION, RENEWAL, AND FUTURE LEADERSHIP

Planning, Ethics, AI, and What Remains

CHAPTER 37:
Falling Out of Rhythm

No matter how seasoned they are, even successful musicians eventually hit stretches where the rhythm slips. Sometimes, it happens slowly, a slight rush in the tempo, a drag in the beat. Other times it arrives all at once, like losing your footing on a familiar path. The notes are the same, but the timing is off. The groove is not gone; it is simply out of reach.

I have seen this kind of integrity in live performance more than once.

At a Blue October concert in Texas, the lead singer

stopped after the first verse of a song. He paused, shook his head slightly, and said something to the effect of, "I love this song, and I just messed it up. Let me start again and do it right for you. You deserve that." There was no defensiveness in his voice. No embarrassment masked as humor. Just responsibility. The band reset. They began again. And the room felt more connected, not less.

I saw something similar at a Goo Goo Dolls concert in Spokane. They launched into "Iris," missed the opening in a way that threw the moment off, laughed, apologized, and began again from the top. What could have been awkward became iconic. The restart did not diminish the song. It made it human.

During her Eras Tour, Taylor Swift has also paused mid-performance to laugh, apologize, adjust, and continue. The scale of the stage did not eliminate fallibility; it revealed composure.

These moments matter. Not because musicians are flawless, but because they model something deeper. When the performance falters, tone determines trust. A restart offered with humility strengthens the bond between performer and audience. It says, "This matters. You matter. Let me do this well."

Leadership carries the same opportunity. When we lose our place, misspeak, rush, or misread the room, we can push forward and hope no one notices. Or we can pause, reset, and begin again with intention.

The restart is rarely about perfection. It is about respect.

There was a season in my career when I felt myself fall out of rhythm. I was not burned out in a dramatic way. I was still showing up, still doing the work, still supporting people. But there was a subtle misalignment, a half-second delay inside me. Conversations felt heavier. Decisions required more effort. Days blurred without their usual sense of meaning.

On the outside, nothing appeared wrong. Inside, the tempo had shifted, and I could not quite find the beat again.

I remember sitting in my office one evening long after everyone else had gone home. School's after-hours carry a quiet that is strangely comforting: the hum of lights, the faint echo of footsteps, the soft click of a door. I was not staying because I needed to. I was staying because I did not know how to end the day. I did not know how to transition from "leader" back to myself.

In that stillness, I finally admitted what I had resisted. I had lost my rhythm. Not permanently. Not catastrophically. But truthfully.

There is a particular humility required to recognize that. Leaders often convince themselves that they must stay composed, keep pace, and carry the room. Slipping out of rhythm can feel like failure, even when it is simply fatigue, even when it is nothing more than being human.

What I needed was not more effort. It was not grit or another late night trying to prove I was in control. What I needed was a pause, and, if I am honest, I also needed encouragement, affirmation that the work mattered, and a chance to feel the purpose again in my body, not just in my job description.

Musicians know that, when they lose the rhythm, they cannot power through blindly and still play the song well. They stop for a beat, listen for the pulse, and re-enter when their body remembers the groove. That pause is not a weakness. It is wisdom.

So, I paused. I closed my laptop. Turned off the light. Walked the hallway slowly, as if learning the building again.

The next morning, I arrived early, not to get ahead, but to breathe. To let the school wake up around me before it asked anything of me. The rhythm did not snap back all at once, but it began to return, soft and low, like a bass line you feel in your ribs before you hear it clearly.

That pause helped me see what I had been missing: the children we serve, the impact we make, the light we help kindle.

What surprised me most was how many people assumed I was fine. Leaders can fall out of rhythm quietly because the pace of the work masks the internal shift. Falling out of rhythm is not failure. It is evidence that you have been carrying too much for too long without taking a break.

Over time, I learned to treat those moments as signals. Messages that something in me needed rest, recalibration, or renewal. Students experience this. Teachers experience this. Leaders experience this. Every human being eventually feels the day grow heavier and the rhythm slip.

The question is not whether it happens. The question is how gently we choose to find our way back.

Falling out of rhythm taught me to lead myself with the same compassion I readily offered to others. It taught me that recovery is not earned. It is allowed. It reminded me that the best leaders are not those who never falter, but those who listen closely enough to notice when they do.

Slowly, steadily, the rhythm will return. Not because you chase it, but because you make space for it. You feel the pulse again. You find your tempo. You re-enter the music, not flawlessly, but honestly.

Sometimes the rhythm you return to is truer than the one you lost.

CHAPTER 38:
The Hardest Conversation

Every leader eventually walks into a room knowing the words they are about to speak will land heavily. There is no musical score to lead you through those moments, no rehearsal that fully prepares you for the convergence of responsibility,

compassion, and consequence. It is the leadership equivalent of performing a song you care about too much to play casually, the one tied to grief, memory, or a truth you cannot soften.

You still must play it, knowing the room will change because you do.

Bands understand this dynamic intimately. Any ensemble that lasts long enough must face the difficult task of addressing what is not working. Sometimes it is a member who cannot stay in time. Sometimes ego overpowers the sound. Sometimes it is a beloved person whose capacity has changed. The conversation is rarely about punishment. It is about stewardship, protecting something larger than one person's comfort.

I once delayed such a conversation longer than I should have.

A thoughtful, respected, deeply committed teacher was unraveling in ways that were beginning to affect children. Lessons became scattered. Responses grew sharp. Students felt unsettled. Colleagues started whispering to one another instead of speaking directly to her. Something needed to be named but entering that conversation felt like stepping into unresolved dissonance.

Here is the strange thing about stress: we often spend more time suffering in the anticipation of a difficult conversation than in the conversation itself.

The longer I delayed, the more my body carried the tension. My sleep lightened. My shoulders tightened. I rehearsed imaginary versions of the meeting, most of them harsher than what would ever occur. Deferred courage accumulates interest.

Eventually, the day arrived.

I remember walking toward her room with my heartbeat rising. The hallway felt too bright, too quiet. She looked up, expecting a light exchange, unaware of what was coming. I wished that were true as well, but leadership does not grant us only easy moments.

We sat. I breathed. I told the truth, not harshly, not clinically, but with clarity and care. I named what I had seen, what students were experiencing, and what others had been unable or afraid to articulate.

Her face did not collapse. It softened.

Tears gathered but did not fall. She nodded, absorbing what she already sensed but could not bring herself to say. Eventually, she whispered, "I knew something was wrong. I just didn't know how to say it out loud."

Sometimes the hardest conversation becomes the opening through which someone finally tells their own truth.

From that point on, there were more meetings, support, accountability, vulnerability, and decisions. None of it was easy. Much of it was relieving. Beneath the sting was a quiet gratitude that someone finally acknowledged what had been happening.

Leadership cultures are no different from bands. Avoidance does not preserve the music. It erodes it. Delay rarely reduces strain. In fact, your nervous system pays the toll of postponed courage. Stress hormones surge, sleep falters, rumination takes over, and the issue grows larger in the mind than it often is in reality. Most of the discomfort leaders carry happens before difficult conversations, not during them.

I have had conversations with parents whose children needed more than the school could provide. I have sat with students whose behavior required intervention. I have had to confront patterns in leaders that were weakening the culture. I have even had conversations with myself, arguably the hardest ones.

Each time, the same paradox shows up: honesty without compassion becomes cruelty, while compassion without honesty becomes avoidance. Leadership asks us to hold both notes at once. Clarity and dignity. Truth and care. The point is not to "win" a conversation. The point is to restore health to the music.

What makes these conversations harder is the temptation to procrastinate. We rationalize delay as kindness or timing. However, delay only increases the emotional cost, to us, to the other person, and to the environment. Avoidance is not mercy. It is prolonged dissonance.

Courage is not found in delivering pain. It is found in honoring reality, so growth can begin.

There is no perfect way to have a hard conversation. Your voice may shake. You may replay the moment afterward, wondering what you could have phrased more gently or more directly. Stepping into the room anyway and staying present through the tension is what allows resolution.

Often, the relief afterward reveals something that is both humbling and freeing: much of what we suffered was generated by our imagination, not by the moment itself.

The hardest conversations reveal who you are, not your title, but your tone. Held well, they transform confrontation into possibility. The room shifts. Change becomes conceivable. Relationships, though altered, can remain intact and respectful.

Sometimes, weeks or years later, you recognize what you could not see in the moment: the conversation you most feared was also the point where the music began to change. Truth finally entered the arrangement, stress loosened its grip, and the song, though disrupted, became clearer, steadier, and more capable of growth.

CHAPTER 39:
When Tone Becomes Distortion

Every profession has them. The abrasive ones. The diminishing ones. The individuals who enter a room and quietly drain whatever steadiness was present. They interrupt to assert relevance, weaponize urgency, and inflate themselves by shrinking others. Their behavior is often rationalized as "high standards," "strong leadership," or "just how they are." Over time, the cost of that rationalization becomes unmistakable.

This dynamic is not confined to schools or organizations; it is just as visible in music. Most bands encounter the individual who disrupts flow under the guise of precision. The one who stops mid-rehearsal to correct others, insisting on technical exactness while their own timing drifts. Their focus is not on creating something responsive and alive, but on replicating something fixed and external. Every note must match. Every phrase must mirror. In doing so, they constrict the very conditions that make music possible: attunement, trust, and shared rhythm. What could have evolved into something original instead collapses under the weight of control.

There is also a more direct form of harm, less disguised and no less corrosive. The "plain old mean." The hand slammed down on the table to punctuate authority. The sharp interruption because "no one can do it right." The persistent micromanagement that leaves no room for growth. These behaviors rarely present as singular events. They accumulate. Over time, they do not elevate performance; they narrow it. People begin to hesitate where they once acted. They defer where they once contributed. Potential is not developed; it is contained.

Leaving an environment shaped by these dynamics is not failure. It is often the moment of recognition that staying is extracting something essential: clarity, confidence, internal rhythm. Walking away is not retreat. It is the reclamation of a tone that took years to develop.

Contemporary research affirms what experienced leaders have long understood intuitively: what occurs in the "invisible" relational spaces of organizations produces measurable outcomes. Persistent incivility, emotional volatility, and contempt, particularly when modeled or tolerated by those in authority, degrade trust, impair cognitive processing, and reduce discretionary effort (Porath & Pearson, 2013). Leadership, in this sense, extends beyond strategy and decision-making. It is a form of relational and embodied stewardship.

This is resonance in its most literal sense. Environments characterized by attunement, steadiness, and dignity do more than improve morale; they support physiological regulation. Conversely, environments marked by unpredictability, humiliation, or chronic threat produce sustained stress responses that alter behavior, perception, and capacity. Trauma research is clear: repeated exposure to destabilizing conditions does not simply pass through individuals; it is internalized, shaping posture, voice, attention, and executive functioning (van der Kolk, 2014). Tone is not an abstraction. It is carried in the body.

There is, however, a corresponding and necessary optimism. Harm leaves residue, but so does care. Each moment of calm under pressure, each boundary held without cruelty, each interaction grounded in dignity contributes to repair. The leader's presence becomes consequential not only in what is decided, but in what is regulated. The echo of leadership is experienced in breath, in attention, and in the degree to which individuals feel able to bring their full capacity to the work.

Some bands fail not because of a deficit of talent, but because the relational conditions required for coherence never stabilize. The history of Oasis offers a visible example. At the height of global success, creative output, and cultural relevance, the band fractured. The issue was not musical capability; it was relational breakdown. Sustained conflict between the Gallagher brothers ultimately rendered collaboration untenable. Even exceptional performance could not compensate for the absence of functional relational infrastructure. Success does not override system failure; it often masks it—until it no longer can.

The implication for leadership is direct. You cannot produce coherent work in a system where listening is absent. You cannot lead effectively in an environment that requires your silence. You cannot maintain professional integrity in conditions that consistently interfere with your capacity to act in alignment with what is right.

Empirical evidence reinforces this pattern. Prolonged exposure to abusive or destructive supervision is associated with increased psychological strain, emotional exhaustion, anxiety, and disengagement. Individuals adapt not by strengthening, but by constricting—muting voice, narrowing judgment, and avoiding risk—because the environment renders authentic engagement costly (Tepper, 2000; Porath & Pearson, 2013).

Not every difficult context necessitates departure. Some situations call for structured accountability, provided the system is capable of protecting truth and enabling repair. However, where harmful behavior is normalized, minimized, or rewarded, accountability mechanisms fail. In such conditions, remaining is not neutral; it becomes participatory. Leaving, therefore, is not avoidance. It is ethical clarity.

There comes a point in both music and leadership when discernment is required. When to continue investing, and when to disengage. When to keep fishing, and when to cut bait. Not every stage is worth preserving. Not every configuration of talent produces coherence. Not every individual in a position of authority functions as a model of leadership.

The primary responsibility is not endurance. It is preservation: of health, of humanity, and of the capacity to lead with integrity. At times, the most consequential leadership decision is not how to remain, but when to step away from a dynamic that distorts both self and system.

Leaving is not defeat. It is release. It is the deliberate removal of what dampens resonance so that what remains can vibrate with clarity. It is the decision to seek, or to build, environments where contribution is not suppressed but amplified.

Sometimes the most important leadership move is simply this: refuse to continue playing in a band that makes everyone worse.

You deserve better music than that.

CHAPTER 40:
Put Down Your Instruments and Plan

Musicians love to play. There is something addictive about picking up an instrument and letting momentum carry you forward. Sound produces energy. Energy produces movement. Movement feels like progress. But the best musicians understand a harder truth: if all you do is play, the music eventually frays. Tempo drifts. Familiar patterns repeat. Volume replaces intention. You are still performing, but you are no longer shaping the sound.

At some point, you have to put down your instrument and plan.

After the success of *The Joshua Tree* and *Rattle and Hum*, U2 reached a moment many bands never recognize. They were successful. Celebrated. Established. And yet something in the sound had grown predictable. Exhausted and crowded by their own image, they resisted the easier path of repeating what had worked. Instead of touring endlessly on momentum, they stepped away. They retreated to Berlin, not to perform, but to dismantle assumptions, argue, experiment, and rethink who they were becoming.

It was uncomfortable. It was messy. It was necessary.

What emerged was *Achtung Baby*, a reinvention that would have been impossible without interruption.

Greatness is not sustained through constant output. It is sustained through an intentional pause.

Leadership in schools faces the same inflection point. Activity multiplies. Initiatives stack. Urgency compounds. Leaders move from one demand to the next, solving problems in real time. The calendar fills. Emails accelerate. Conversations overlap. Momentum creates the illusion of effectiveness.

But motion is not clarity.

There are seasons when working harder deepens confusion. Conversations repeat without resolution. Competing priorities sit side by side without hierarchy. Fatigue is misread as resistance. Escalation is driven less by malice than by misalignment. Leaders respond by increasing output, holding another meeting, issuing another directive, or making another revision, yet the sound does not improve.

Because the issue is not effort. It is coherence.

For a stretch of my own career, I led like a professional Whack-A-Mole player, sprinting from crisis to crisis. Those roles matter in certain seasons. Schools need leaders who can steady a room, absorb anxiety, and act quickly. But when urgency becomes the culture, strategy disappears. Improvisation without intention turns into reactivity. You perform the music rather than compose the set.

I reached a point when I realized I was always "on." I could soothe tension. I could respond quickly. I could carry weight. But I was not shaping the long arc. I was reacting to noise rather than listening for direction. The days were full, yet the direction felt thin.

The shift came during a retreat I did not want to attend. Stepping into quiet felt irresponsible, almost indulgent. How could I justify pause when so much needed attention? But once the noise fell away, something unexpected happened. Clarity returned, not the clarity of immediate answers, but the clarity of better questions.

What matters most right now?
What needs to grow?
What needs to end?
What am I reinforcing simply by repetition?

Those questions had been inaccessible while I was strumming continuously.

Putting down your instrument and planning is a reflection during complexity. It is not preparation before action, that work belongs to readiness. It is recalibration within action. It is the discipline of interrupting momentum long enough to determine whether the work still aligns with its purpose.

In one particularly compressed academic year, our leadership team was navigating curriculum reform, staffing shifts, and rising community tension simultaneously. Every issue was legitimate. Every meeting felt necessary. Yet progress slowed. We were engaged constantly, but not coherently. The breakthrough did not come from pushing harder. It came when we cleared an agenda and asked one anchoring question: What must remain true for us regardless of pressure?

The room quieted. People leaned back. Priorities sharpened. Energy realigned. We had stopped long enough to hear the song again.

Planning is not retreat. It is recalibration.

It is not primarily about spreadsheets or timelines. It is about coherence, aligning purpose, people, and practice. In schools especially, planning is an ethical act. Every decision echoes into classrooms and homes. When leaders plan with care, they reduce unintended harm, increase trust, and create conditions where others can lead responsibly.

Putting down your instrument also models restraint. It signals that leadership is not constant performance. It gives others permission to think rather than react. It shifts culture from volume to direction.

Eventually, you pick the instrument back up. But you play differently. The tempo steadies. The song simplifies. What emerges is not louder leadership, but truer leadership, one that understands cadence. One that knows when to push and when to pause. One that recognizes that reinvention requires room.

Sometimes the most powerful leadership decision you can make is the simplest:

Stop.
Step back.
Look at the map.
Decide where the music needs to go.

Then pick up your instrument again, intentional, aligned, and ready.

CHAPTER 41:
Rocking in the Free World: Leadership in the Age of AI

Every generation of musicians faces a moment when the tools of their craft change. Electric guitars once felt like a threat to tradition. Synthesizers were dismissed as gimmicks. Looping pedals, sampling machines, reverb layers, distortion engines, chorus effects, and sound-emulating amplifiers were all accused of cheapening talent rather than expanding it. Auto-tune was mocked as fraud before artists turned it into its own expressive language. Today, even songwriting can be augmented, chord progressions suggested by software, lyrics nudged by algorithms, tracks mastered by listening models trained on millions of songs.

Synthesizers, electric guitars, and looping machines did not kill the music. They allowed it to evolve.

The truth has remains constant across every wave of innovation: tools don't create meaning; people do.

A great musician can move a room with nothing but an unplugged guitar, a voice, a few honest chords, and something true to say. That same musician can electrify a stadium with a wall of sound built on pedals, processors, and effects. The technology shapes the texture. The heart shapes the impact.

Artificial intelligence is simply the newest instrument in the room.

Some leaders greet it with excitement. Others with suspicion. Many are in fear. All of these reactions make sense because AI arrives like a new bandmate no one auditioned who somehow already knows every part. It harmonizes instantly. It drafts, analyzes, synthesizes, reorganizes, translates, and predicts, often faster than we can keep up. It expands capacity in ways that feel disorienting precisely because they are new.

Used well, AI does not replace the human tone. It amplifies it.

Like a reverb pedal, it can widen a voice, but it does not give it soul. Like delay, it can thicken a line, but it does not give it intention. The first time I used an AI tool professionally, I felt a strange mix of awe and discomfort. It was fast, startlingly fast, and a part of me wondered if I was handing something essential away. When I stepped back, though, the distinction became clear: the tool could generate material, but it could not select meaning. It could mimic tone, but it could not create truth. It could assist the work, but it could not carry responsibility.

Leadership remains personal.

Ethan Mollick (2023) describes AI not as an autopilot, but as a co-intelligence or "co-pilot", a powerful assistant that expands thinking, accelerates drafts, and surfaces options, while leaving judgment, ethics, and final decisions firmly in human hands. Used well, AI reduces cognitive load so leaders can focus on distinctly human capacities: discernment, moral reasoning, and relational presence.

Global guidance echoes this distinction. UNESCO (2023) emphasizes in its *Guidance for Generative AI in Education and Research* that human agency, dignity, and accountability must remain central. AI may support learning, planning, and system design, but it cannot replace human judgment, care, or ethical responsibility.

This is the leadership line that matters.

Just as musicians learned that amplifier modeling did not kill authenticity but broadened sound, leaders must learn that AI does not eclipse their role. It clarifies it. Our value is no longer in being faster than a machine. It is about being more human than one.

In this new landscape, presence matters more. Tone matters more. Listening matters more. Integrity matters far more.

Students do not look to algorithms for safety, courage, or belonging. Colleagues do not trust systems to make ethical decisions when the stakes are human. They look to people, people who walk into rooms with steadiness, wisdom, and heart. AI can tune a voice, but it cannot build trust, because trust forms in the slow, uncertain work of showing up for someone over time. It can draft a letter, but it cannot repair a relationship. It can generate options, but it cannot sit with disappointment, grief, or fear.

Those remain human tasks.

I often picture a musician onstage with a row of pedals, delay, reverb, distortion, looping, sampling. Each expands possibility, but none can replace the soul behind the strings. Musicians who rely solely on effects without craft are exposed quickly. Audiences can sense when sound is engineered, but the heart is absent.

AI is a digital pedalboard. Powerful. Versatile. Transformative. The tone still has to come from you.

The leaders who will thrive in this era are not those who fear the tool, nor those who worship it. They are the ones who integrate it thoughtfully, using it to clear noise, widen bandwidth, sharpen insight, and create more space for the work that only humans can do.

Education, at its core, is relational. Leadership, at its core, is moral. Safeguarding, at its core, is human protection.

No algorithm can read the silence in a room. No system can notice the subtle way a child withdraws. No model can hold a boundary with compassion while staying present to someone's pain. AI can assist the work, but it cannot be the work.

We are still, all of us, rocking in the free world, not because the world is easy, but because it is open. Open to new tools. Open to reinvention. Open to expanded capacity. Freedom requires responsibility. In this era, the responsibility is to lead with greater humanity, not less.

So, yes, use the tools. Invite them into the band. Let them stretch what you can do. Never forget, though: the tone is yours. The voice is yours. The judgment, the courage, the conscience, those remain human.

AI may harmonize with you, but it cannot take the stage in your place.

CHAPTER 42:
The Hidden Track That Holds It All Together

In leadership, we talk endlessly about strategy, culture, vision, systems, and resilience. We analyze the chords we play, the tone we set, and the crowds we hope to lift. There is one element of leadership that rarely appears in frameworks or professional diagrams, and yet, it may be the most important of all: the person who stands with you when the stage lights burn hot, and the music falters.

The person who shares your life is the hidden track beneath the song. The quiet amplifier backstage. The one who keeps you in tune when the world only hears the melody you project.

Leadership is public, performative, and often unforgiving. Partnership, when it is real, is private, steady, and unrelenting in its care. It is the safety net under the high wire. The hand at your back when confidence wavers. The place where you land when the notes come out wrong.

I have been fortunate to live inside that kind of partnership for more than thirty years. Through career shifts, school crises, midnight decisions, and the long, invisible labor of international leadership, my spouse has been the constant rhythm beneath the verse. Their love never depended on whether I got the chord progression right that day. When the music soured, when I made the wrong call, or when the work cracked something inside me, they held space with a steadiness that made repair possible.

There is also a particular kind of feedback that only someone who truly loves you can give. Not flattery, not indulgence, but truth delivered without humiliation. Over the years, my partner has learned how to tell me what I needed to hear, even when I resisted hearing it, without diminishing me. Grace, when I deserved critique. Critique wrapped in grace, when I needed honesty more than comfort. That is a rare gift. It tunes not just the instrument, but the musician.

Leadership can be profoundly lonely, even when you are surrounded by people. Decisions carry weight. Consequences ripple outward. The role itself can begin to eclipse the person inside it. Having someone who sees you beyond the title, who recognizes the human underneath the responsibility, keeps you from becoming an instrument you no longer recognize. Partnership preserves the person so the leader can endure.

In music, harmony emerges when two notes hold tension and resonance together. A single note can be strong, but harmony adds depth, warmth, and durability. Leadership works the same way. You may carry the melody, but partnership sustains the sound. Without it, the music thins. With it, the song can hold weight without breaking.

If there is a final lesson in a life of leadership, it may be this: you were never meant to carry the load alone. We speak often about teams, mentors, and coaches, and they matter. But sometimes the most consequential leader in your story is the one with no professional title, no office, and no audience. The one who loves you enough to keep you grounded, honest, and whole.

That is the power chord underneath everything.

For some of us, for me, it has been the most important one of all.

“I puke quite a lot before going on stage.”

Adele

CHAPTER 43:
Face the Music

There comes a moment in every leader's life when performance is no longer enough.

The room is watching. The decision has landed. The consequences are real. The air changes. Voices lower. Emails arrive with sharper edges. You feel it before anyone names it.

Something has happened.
Something you decided.
Something you allowed.
Something you missed.

In that moment, you are not leading in rehearsal. You are leading under visibility.

Musicians know this moment well. At Live Aid in 1985, when the global broadcast faltered and equipment cut out, performers had seconds to decide whether to panic, blame, or steady themselves. There is no hiding when millions are watching. A wrong note rings louder in an arena than in a garage. A forgotten lyric does not disappear into rehearsal space. Under lights, mistakes are magnified.

Leadership under consequence feels the same. When a safeguarding decision must be made that implicates a well-liked staff member, when a long-standing tradition is disrupted for equity reasons, or when a misjudgment harms trust, there is no neutral posture. You cannot retreat into abstraction. You cannot soften impact with eloquence alone. The community is watching not only what you decide, but how you inhabit the aftermath.

I once faced a moment that tested this more than I expected. A concern was raised about a respected adult in our community. The allegation was not yet proven. It was not yet public. But it was serious enough to require immediate action. Policy was clear. The emotional cost was not.

Suspending someone people admire is not theoretical. It is visible. It shakes hallways. It creates fear. It generates rumor. It invites resistance.

In that moment, I could have delayed. I could have sought quiet compromise. I could have minimized the concern in the name of stability. Instead, we followed the procedure precisely. We communicated carefully. We absorbed the backlash.

The decision protected students. It also costs relational capital.

The harder part came after the announcement. Questions sharpened. Motives were speculated about. I was asked directly if I had overreacted. The temptation was subtle: defend the process with authority, retreat behind confidentiality, emphasize my experience.

But facing the music required something different. It required standing visibly in the discomfort and saying, calmly, "This is difficult. It affects people we care about. And our responsibility to student safety is not negotiable."

That sentence did not end the tension. It anchored it. Leadership under tension is not about emotional control alone. It is about moral steadiness. There are moments when a leader's silence protects reputation but harms integrity. There are moments when clarity invites criticism but safeguards principle. The difference between those choices defines culture.

I have also faced moments when the music was mine to own.

A communication sent too quickly. A decision framed poorly. A tone that carried unintended sharpness. In those instances, the instinct to explain is powerful. Context is easy to construct. Justification is readily available. But explanation without ownership erodes trust.

There was a season when I made a call intended to stabilize a situation quickly. It did. In the short term, it solved the problem in front of me. In the longer term, it sidelined voices that deserved more space. Efficiency had replaced listening. What I saw as decisiveness, others experienced as dismissal.

When the feedback came, it would have been easy to say, "You're misunderstanding my intent." Instead, I said what felt far more exposed: "I moved too quickly. I should have slowed down and invited more voices in. That's on me."

Ownership did not erase the impact. But it changed the trajectory of trust.

Teams do not expect perfection. They expect congruence. Students do not require infallibility. They require safety. Communities can endure difficult decisions. They fracture under defensiveness.

Facing the music is the discipline of remaining present when the cost becomes visible. It is standing in consequence without collapsing into shame or escalating into control. It is absorbing scrutiny without weaponizing authority. Without this string, the chord is incomplete.

Preparation matters. Reflection matters. Empathy matters. But when something breaks under public light, none of those qualities substitute for ownership. This is the string that tests the others. It asks whether your preparation was real, whether your reflection was honest, and whether your empathy extends to those disappointed by you.

Leadership under visibility reveals what private leadership only suggests.

It is easy to speak about values in a planning session. It is harder to uphold them when they are unpopular. It is easy to champion transparency until transparency exposes you. It is easy to encourage growth until growth requires apology.

Facing the music is not about dramatic confession. It is about consistent congruence.

The most powerful leadership decision you may ever make will not be innovative or strategic. It will be ethical. It will be the decision to say, "I was wrong," or "This is the right call, even if it costs us," or "We will absorb this tension because it protects what matters most."

Musicians understand that tension is not the enemy of sound. It is the source of resonance. A string too loose produces nothing. A string too tight snaps. Leadership lives in that narrow band where tension is held with integrity.

The lights will come on.
The room will watch.
The consequences will land.

The question is simple and relentless: Who are you when everyone can see the impact of your leadership?

The music does not resolve because the audience is pleased. It resolves because someone stays steady long enough for the note to settle. Face the music. Stand in consequence. Let integrity hold the tension until trust finds its way back into the room.

Then begin again… not louder, but truer.

CHAPTER 44:
Resonance: What Remains After the Last Note

A song does not end with its final note. Even after the audience grows quiet and the lights soften, something lingers. The air still carries vibration. The sound settles slowly into the room, almost imperceptibly, but undeniably present. That lingering is resonance, the part of the music that outlives the performance itself.

Leadership has resonance, too.

Meetings end. School years close. Students graduate. Roles change. Offices empty. Systems evolve. Yet something of your tone stays behind. Not the agenda. Not the slide deck. Not even the decision in its technical form. What remains is subtler than that. It is the felt experience of having been led by you.

Leadership is never neutral. Presence teaches long before instruction begins. People are always observing how you respond under pressure, how you greet them when no one influential is watching, how you handle mistakes, your own and theirs. They notice how you speak to those who cannot advance your career and how you carry yourself when outcomes are uncertain. Over time, those moments accumulate. They become climate.

Years after leaving one school, I returned as a visitor. The paint was new. The faces had changed. The systems were updated. And yet something felt familiar. It was not ownership, and it certainly was not credit. It was an echo, in the way adults spoke to students, in the steadiness of meetings, in how disagreement was handled without performance or defensiveness. Tone had outlived tenure.

That is resonance.

You do not control it completely, but you contribute to it continuously.

Most leaders overestimate the impact of their most visible moments and underestimate the power of their smallest ones. A calm response in a tense exchange. A boundary held with dignity rather than volume. An apology offered without qualification. A conversation treated as worthy of unhurried attention. These are the notes that carry.

Once, a former student told me she remembered none of the content I taught. What she remembered was that I listened without rushing and that she felt taken seriously. That presence shaped her more than any objective ever could. It was a humbling reminder that tone becomes curriculum.

Long after your last note fades, your sound will still be teaching.

And if you listen carefully, you can hear what shaped it. Emotional range, the willingness to live in both high notes and low ones without pretending. Harmony is the discipline of aligning differences rather than demanding uniformity. Awareness, the humility to read the room before attempting to lead it. Readiness, the responsibility of preparing yourself before stepping forward. Reflection is the courage to interrupt momentum when coherence begins to slip.

Accountability, the steadiness to stand visibly in consequence without retreating into defensiveness.

These are not abstract metaphors. They are lived practices. Each carries tension. Each requires tuning. Together, they form the sound of a leader whose presence leaves rooms steadier than they found them.

Resonance is not accidental. It is cumulative. You do not build it in a single performance or in one defining decision. You build it across a thousand ordinary moments, in how you respond, how you repair, how you listen, how you hold tension without breaking it.

Eventually, every leader walks off stage. Titles fade. Applause quiets. Programs evolve. What remains is not the volume of your leadership but the vibration it left behind.

The question is not whether something will remain. Something always does.

The question is what kind of hum the room holds when you leave.

If you have tuned all six strings, if you have led with range, alignment, awareness, preparation, reflection, and integrity, the echo will not be loud. It will be steady.

And steady leadership is what endures.

ENCORE:
Play the Note That Is Yours

Every concert must eventually come to an end. The lights dim. The final chord dissolves into the room. Applause rises, then settles into a waiting hush. The band steps offstage.

The audience stays. The encore lives in that pause.

Encores are complicated things. What is an encore, really? Is it a gift, or a ritual? Generosity, or choreography? Is the band returning because the audience called them back, or because the pause was always part of the design?

As David Byrne (2012) observes in *How Music Works*, many rituals of live performance, including encores, are far less spontaneous than audiences imagine. What feels like a moment of pure generosity is often carefully constructed anticipation.

The audience has already paid. The music is already owed. So, why the ritual? Why the pause? Why the demand for more applause before offering what everyone knows is coming?

It is an uncomfortable question, because sometimes the answer is ego.

Sometimes, though, the answer is sincerity.

A false encore is about control. It extracts affirmation. It extends attention. It feeds fragile importance. It treats the audience as a mirror rather than a partner.

A true encore is something else entirely. It is not performed because it is demanded. It is offered because something genuine remains.

Leadership has encores, too.

There is the performative encore, staying visible, staying relevant, staying applauded. Then, there is the quieter, truer one: the leadership you continue offering when no one is watching, when the title has faded, when authority has been handed off.

That is not about applause. That is about integrity. The real encore is not the last chance to be seen. It is the moment you choose to remain who you are.

Over time, I realized that many of my most meaningful leadership moments did not happen on the main stage. They happened afterward, in the way I still made careful decisions without being required to, in the care I extended when it no longer benefited me, in the tone I carried into rooms where I had no formal role.

Somewhere along the way, leadership stopped being something I did and became something I practiced, quietly, consistently, without an audience.

That is the true encore. It is not about playing your greatest hits. It is about playing your truest note.

The one shaped by experience and loss, by humility and conviction, by care that no longer needs recognition.

Leadership, like musicianship, is not a single performance. It is a lifetime of tuning and retuning. You miss the beat. You find it again. You learn when to lead and when to listen. You discover, often late, that the most powerful moments are not the loudest ones.

The encore that matters is not the one that proves you were great.
It is the one that proves you were real.

That is why some final offerings linger long after the lights go down. Not because they were dramatic, but because they were honest. Not because they demanded attention, but because they carried truth.

When someone keeps offering their best, not to be praised, not to be relevant, not to be remembered, but simply because it is who they are, the sound changes.

The room feels it.

At this stage of life, I think less about stages and more about tone. Less about being heard and more about being aligned. The world does not need more performance. It needs presence. It needs people who will keep playing the note that is theirs, not for applause, not for legacy, not for proof, but because the music is not finished inside them.

Play it boldly or quietly.
Play it in crowded rooms or empty ones.
Play it when you are confident and when you are unsure.
Play it when no one is asking for more.

Every leader has an encore. The only question that matters is this:
Will it be an act of ego, or an act of generosity?

When you play the note that is truly yours, the room will know the difference.

Long after the applause fades, it will still resonate.

FINAL CHORD: PLAYING UNDER TENSION

Leadership, like music, is not built on complexity alone. It is built on a few essential disciplines, practiced until they can be relied on in the moment when the moment demands it.

The Power Chords are these:

- **High Notes and Low Notes**: Expand your range. Lead across emotional registers without losing authenticity.
- **Harmony**: Align differences. Listen, adjust, and create coherence without forcing sameness.
- **Know Your Audience**: Read before you respond. Influence begins with awareness.
- **Set Up Your Own Gear**: Prepare yourself. Show up grounded, clear, and ready.
- **Put Down Your Instruments and Plan**: Interrupt the noise. Pause long enough to restore direction.
- **Face the Music**: Stand in the moment. Own decisions when visibility and consequence arrive.

Individually, **each string matters.** Together, they form a way of leading that holds under pressure.

Leadership does not happen in controlled conditions. It happens in real time, in shifting environments, in moments that do not wait. In those moments, you do not live up to your intentions. You return to the level of your practice.

Each string carries tension. That tension is not a flaw. It is what allows the chord to hold.

In the end, leadership is not defined by how well you understand these ideas. It is defined by whether you can play them consistently under pressure, when it counts.

Pick up the instrument. Tune it. And play.

Who is your conductor?

Musician	Influence	Summary
Paul McCartney	Buddy Holly	McCartney has frequently cited Holly as a formative influence on songwriting and band structure.
Jimi Hendrix	Chas Chandler	Chandler discovered Hendrix and played a critical role in launching his career.
Bruce Springsteen	Jon Landau	Landau became both producer and intellectual mentor, shaping Springsteen's artistic direction.
Billie Eilish	Finneas O'Connell	Finneas has served as primary collaborator and creative architect behind her early work.
Taylor Swift	Shania Twain / Faith Hill	Swift has credited both artists with shaping her early crossover country-pop identity.
Elton John	Bernie Taupin	Taupin's lyrics formed the foundation of Elton John's catalog.
Ed Sheeran	Eric Clapton	Sheeran has cited Clapton as a key reason he began playing guitar.
Beyoncé	Tina Turner	Beyoncé has named Turner as a model of performance power and stage presence.
Dave Grohl	Lemmy Kilmister	Grohl has spoken publicly about Lemmy's influence on his approach to rock authenticity.
John Mayer	Stevie Ray Vaughan	Mayer has consistently described Vaughan as a central guitar influence.
Lady Gaga	Elton John / David Bowie	Gaga has acknowledged both as influences on artistic identity and theatricality.
Bono	Bob Dylan	Bono has cited Dylan's lyrical depth as formative.
Slash	Joe Perry	Slash has named Perry as an early guitar hero.
Whitney Houston	Aretha Franklin	Houston regarded Franklin as a vocal and artistic model.
Adele	Ella Fitzgerald	Adele has referenced Fitzgerald as an influence on phrasing and tone.
Keith Richards	Chuck Berry	Richards has openly credited Berry's riffs and style as foundational.

References

Blake, M. (2011). *Comfortably Numb: The Inside Story of Pink Floyd.* Da Capo Press.

Byrne, D. (2012). *How Music Works*. McSweeney's.

Cain, S. (2012). *Quiet: The Power of Introverts in a World That Can't Stop Talking*. Crown Publishing Group.

Caillat, K., & Stiefel, S. (2012). *Making Rumors: The Inside Story of the Classic Fleetwood Mac Album*. Wiley.

Davis, S. (2017). *Gold Dust Woman: The Biography of Stevie Nicks*. St. Martin's Press.

Delanceyplace. (2017, March 7). *John Lennon struggled with performance nerves*. https://delanceyplace.com

Hattie, J. (2012). *Visible learning for teachers: Maximizing impact on learning*. Routledge.

Maxwell, J. C. (2007). *The 21 Irrefutable Laws of Leadership: Follow Them and People Will Follow You* (10th anniversary ed.). Thomas Nelson.

Mabbett, A. (2010). *Pink Floyd: The Music and the Mystery*. Omnibus Press.

Neville, M. (Director). (2013). *20 Feet from Stardom* [Documentary film]. Tremolo Productions.

Nicks, S. (1981). *Interview on songwriting and inspiration* [Television interview]. Reiterated in *In Your Dreams* [Documentary film]. (2011). Reprise Records.

Nicks, S. (1998). *VH1 Behind the Music: Fleetwood Mac* [Television documentary]. VH1 Productions.

Mollick, E. (2023). *Co-intelligence: Living and working with AI.* Portfolio.

Porath, C., & Pearson, C. (2013). "The Price of Incivility." *Harvard Business Review, 91*(1–2), 115–121.

Tepper, B. J. (2000). "Consequences of Abusive Supervision." *Academy of Management Journal, 43*(2), 178–190.

Van der Kolk, B. A. (2014). *The Body Keeps the Score: Brain, Mind, and Body in the Healing of Trauma.* Viking.

UNESCO. (2023). *Guidance for generative AI in education and research.* UNESCO Publishing

"Every night, we're trying to prove we belong on that stage."

Bruce Springsteen

www.ingramcontent.com/pod-product-compliance
Lightning Source LLC
LaVergne TN
LVHW010653110826
845149LV00014B/3065

9780989780551